Climate Change Policy:
Challenging the Activists

Climate Change Policy: Challenging the Activists

EDITED BY COLIN ROBINSON

iea

The Institute of Economic Affairs

First published in Great Britain in 2008 by
The Institute of Economic Affairs
2 Lord North Street
Westminster
London SW1P 3LB
in association with Profile Books Ltd

The mission of the Institute of Economic Affairs is to improve public understanding of the fundamental institutions of a free society, by analysing and expounding the role of markets in solving economic and social problems.

A CIP catalogue record for this book is available from the British Library.

ISBN 978 0 255 36595 6

Many IEA publications are translated into languages other than English or are reprinted. Permission to translate or to reprint should be sought from the Director General at the address above.

Typeset in Stone by MacGuru Ltd
info@macguru.org.uk

Printed and bound in Great Britain by Hobbs the Printers

CONTENTS

THE AUTHORS

Ian Byatt

Sir Ian Byatt is Chairman of the Water Industry Commission for Scotland and a Senior Associate at Frontier Economics. He was Director-General of Water Services (Ofwat) from the privatisation of the Water Authorities in 1989 to 2000, setting up the regulatory office and developing the new regime. He was previously head of the Public Sector Economic Unit and then Deputy Chief Economic Adviser at HM Treasury, where he was engaged in the reform of supply-side policy. Before entering government service he taught at Durham University and the London School of Economics. He works closely with the Public Utility Research Center at the University of Florida.

David Henderson

David Henderson is formerly head of the Department of Economics and Statistics at the OECD and is currently a Visiting Professor at the Westminster Business School, London. He has written a number of IEA publications, including *Misguided Virtue* – an investigation into the corporate social responsibility agenda. He is also a member of the IEA's Academic Advisory Council.

Russell Lewis

Russell Lewis is a veteran campaigner for political and economic freedom who has always been ready to defy majority opinion. In 1968 he put forward in the *Daily Telegraph* detailed proposals for wholesale denationalisation by selling shares in public concerns to the people. In 1971 his IEA monograph *Rome or Brussels* spelt out the danger of a superstate Europe run by unelected bureaucrats. In 1973, in his book *The New Service Society*, he showed that the economic future lay with the services, not, as pop economists like G. K. Galbraith were arguing, with the likes of General Motors. His ten or so books include the first biography of Margaret Thatcher – a best-seller. His more recent publication *Global Warming: False Alarms* is available to be downloaded from the IEA website (www. iea.org.uk).

Julian Morris

Julian Morris is Executive Director of the International Policy Network (www.policynetwork.net) and a Visiting Professor at the University of Buckingham. Prior to founding IPN, he was Director of the Environment and Technology Programme at the IEA, where he wrote and edited numerous books, monographs and papers, including *Global Warming: Apocalypse or Hot Air?* (with Roger Bate, 1994) and *Global Warming: Challenging the Conventional Wisdom* (1997). Julian has various Masters degrees in economics and related disciplines, as well as a graduate diploma in law. He is co-editor, with Dr Indur Goklany, of the *Electronic Journal of Sustainable Development* (www.ejsd.org), and a member of the editorial board of *Energy and Environment.* A Fellow of the Royal Society of Arts, he is on the Council of the School of Pharmacy

(London) and on the Academic Advisory Council of the IEA, as well as being on the boards of several other think tanks.

Alan Peacock

Allegedly retired, Sir Alan Peacock, a Fellow of the British Academy and erstwhile Chief Economic Adviser to the Department of Trade and Industry, now holds honorary appointments as Professor of Economics at the Universities of York and Heriot-Watt. He has previously been Vice-Chancellor of the University of Buckingham, a professor at four UK universities and was chairman of the Home Office Committee on the Funding of the BBC (1985–86). In 1985 he co-founded the David Hume Institute, Edinburgh, becoming its first Director (1985–91). In 2002 he was awarded the Royal Medal of the Royal Society of Edinburgh.

Colin Robinson

Colin Robinson worked for eleven years as a business economist, mainly in the oil industry, before being appointed in 1968 to the Chair of Economics at the University of Surrey, where he founded the Department of Economics and is now Emeritus Professor. He is a Fellow of the Royal Statistical Society, of the Society of Business Economists and of the Institute of Energy. In 1998 he received from the International Association for Energy Economics its 'Outstanding Contribution to the Profession and its Literature' award. From 1992 to 2002 he was Editorial Director of the Institute of Economic Affairs, in addition to his university post. He is a member of the IEA's Academic Advisory Council.

FOREWORD

Politicians and their advisers claim to know so much nowadays. For example, they seem to know, for decades ahead:

- the precise relationship between atmospheric concentrations of greenhouse gases (GHGs) and climatic conditions, at global and local scales;
- the extent of positive and negative climatological feedback loops and where the tipping points lie;
- the impacts of non-anthropogenic climatological forces, such as solar and volcanic activity;
- how our economies will progress (including, presumably, the course of events, both human and natural, that will influence that progress);
- the quantities and costs of our resources;
- what every energy-production, energy-storage, energy-transmission and energy-consumption technology will cost and contribute;
- what the contribution will be of technologies not yet invented and resources not yet discovered;
- how the preferences and ways of life of people around the world will develop;
- the profile of the optimum balance in each year between mitigating the risk of harm from climate change through the

constraint of emissions of GHGs, and adapting to reduce the impact of any such harm;

- how much each country should contribute to the mitigation profile;
- the share within the mitigation profile of emissions from the use of energy for heat, transport and electricity;
- for each of those uses, the cost and contribution of each technology;
- how the mitigation profile can most fairly be shared between each industrial and commercial sector (and, in many cases, each site or operator), homes and personal transport, and the public sector;
- and very many other things, in the environmental field and in every other walk of life.

Certainly, the public pronouncements of politicians and the detailed central planning and regulations that they propose seem predicated upon the belief that politicians, their advisers and their regulators have limitless knowledge about the science and economics of climate change, energy use and the environment.

Or perhaps the political class does not have such knowledge, but nevertheless the precautionary principle demands that *something must be done*. That is the asymmetric precautionary principle, which demands precaution against the risk that today's freedoms may harm future generations more than they benefit present generations, but opposes precaution against the risk that today's constraints may harm present generations more than they benefit future generations.

Mechanisms that allow the market to discover the most efficient balance of mitigation and adaptation – and the most efficient ways of achieving that balance – fall foul of this principle. We cannot have the flexibility and impartial apportionment of price rationing. We must have the inflexibility and managed apportionment of state rationing – caps, plans, allocations and (to make it look a little less socialist) a legitimised black market for the excess scraps from the allocations. And this approach to carbon pricing is backed up by a regime of detailed regulation and special taxes and subsidies, not just in relation to energy generation but in relation to a whole range of economic activities.

State rationing needs firm numbers. The uncertainty may be vast and the permutations of all the unknown variables impossibly complex, but we can provide the necessary figures by applying statistical techniques to sets of tenuous assumptions. The probability of future developments conforming with these assumptions may be negligible, but (having rejected a genuine market approach) there is no option to do without assumptions, and any other set of assumptions will be equally improbable. In a few steps, we convert uncertainty into certainty and dictate that our critics must do the same.

Thanks to this certainty, there is no need or space for entrepreneurs in the traditional sense – that is, those who discover new information in the economic process. Governments have worked out the reasonable costs and expected volumes of each technology (or good), and how much each sector of industry and society will contribute (or require), so there is no need for innovation nor opportunity for the unconventional. The job of business is to deliver as cheaply as possible what governments have specified. Without rewards for innovation – for betting against the crowd and winning – the economy coalesces around large businesses with low financial costs, high volumes and low margins delivering

13

what governments have ensured will be the most financially viable (though not necessarily the most economic) solutions.

We do not need to nationalise or regulate to have a centrally planned economy. We can do it just as effectively with incentives. The successful 'entrepreneur' is no longer someone who innovates to provide, more efficiently than the competition, the goods that people want, but someone who has persuaded government to back his version of the future.

According to Bertrand Russell, 'the whole problem with the world is that fools and fanatics are always so certain of themselves, but wiser people so full of doubts'. Unfortunately, we expect our politicians to have all the answers, and our politicians expect likewise from their advisers. So we get the policies we deserve, prescribed by fools and fanatics. Fortunately, there are still a few wise people engaged in the policy debate, and the views of several of them are collected here. Their caution against policy activism in the area of climate change urgently needs to be considered by all those involved in this area.

In the wake of James Hansen's recent call for senior oil-company executives to be prosecuted for 'high crimes against humanity and nature', there is more need than ever for an exploration of the case for reasonable doubt and of the policy prescriptions that flow from acknowledging that doubt.[1]

BRUNO PRIOR

Director, Summerleaze Ltd[2]

July 2008

---

1   *www.guardian.co.uk/environment/2008/jun/23/fossilfuels.climatechange.*

2   Summerleaze Ltd have been renewable energy entrepreneurs since the early 1980s and have been 'beneficiaries' of successive governments' complex and partial interventions.

The views expressed in this monograph are, as in all IEA publications, those of the authors and not those of the Institute (which has no corporate view), its managing trustees, Academic Advisory Council members or senior staff.

TABLE

**Climate Change Policy:
Challenging the Activists**

1 CLIMATE CHANGE AND THE MARKET ECONOMY: INTRODUCTION

Colin Robinson

In *The Affluent Society* (1958: ch. 2), John Kenneth Galbraith coined the term 'conventional wisdom', which he described as 'the name for the ideas which are esteemed at any time for their acceptability'. Galbraith went on to point out that, since exposition of the conventional wisdom 'has the approval of those to whom it is addressed', it is always in great demand and 'it follows that a very large part of our social comment – and nearly all that is well regarded – is devoted at any time to articulating the conventional wisdom'. The conventional wisdom is regarded as 'more or less identical with sound scholarship' and 'its position is virtually impregnable'.

Whatever one's view of Galbraith's work, his notion of the conventional wisdom – ideas notable not for their intellectual content but because they have become acceptable and are what people want to hear – is a powerful one when considering views about climate change. The prevailing view that damaging climate change is in progress and will become worse in the future is perhaps the prime example of the conventional wisdom of the early 21st century. Clearly it is an idea which, in Galbraith's words, is 'esteemed for its acceptability': it is what many people want to hear and so has the approval of those to whom it is addressed. Its exponents are regarded as sound scholars. Leaders of the movement (for such it is) assure their followers and anyone who will listen that 'the science is settled'. Those leaders are indeed so settled in their own beliefs that, in an echo of earlier times, as Sir Alan Peacock explains in Chapter 6 of this volume, they have in recent years tried to silence counter-views and suppress dissent: the only debate they want is about choice among the different forms of the centralised action they believe is required to deal with the problems they foresee.

As always, the conventional wisdom is spread, and its pre-eminence is maintained, by 'intellectuals', most of whom, as Hayek (1949) pointed out, are essentially 'second hand dealers in ideas' rather than original thinkers. Prominent among today's second-hand dealers are the numerous members of the media who provide comment on contemporary issues, who can generally be relied on to support the conventional wisdom. Almost all of them appear to embrace the view that immediate and drastic government action is required to offset damaging climate change. Their general line is that it is obvious that damaging climate change is under way and that it is the duty of people (generally other people) to change their lifestyles, particularly away from activities once thought liberating but now regarded as damaging, such as air and motor vehicle travel. The media tend to support the leaders of the movement, treating the arguments of the relatively few dissenters as though they had little substance. The activities of the media therefore reinforce the position of this piece of conventional wisdom, rendering it, in Galbraith's phrase, 'virtually impregnable'.

But does the damaging climate change hypothesis have the other characteristic implied by Galbraith's analysis of the conventional wisdom? Is it no more than the repetition of ideas that people want to hear and essentially empty of intellectual content?

Or could it be more soundly based and able to cope with changing economic and scientific ideas?

In this monograph six economists write about the damaging climate change hypothesis. They are concerned not to produce yet more models of prospective climate change and its effects but to place the hypothesis in historical context and to consider whether or not its exponents have made their case that urgent, large-scale, centralised action is required to save the world from damaging change in the future. All are sceptical of the case but all are concerned to avoid what they regard as the intolerance of their opponents: they are careful not to go to the other extreme of denying that there is or can be a climate change 'problem'. The world's climate is constantly changing and there are circumstances in which change might become damaging. But they point out some of the lessons of history, they highlight the limitations of government and international action, and they remind their readers of the adaptive capacity of market-based economic systems. One of their principal concerns is that large-scale centralised action to combat the supposed 'threat' of global climate change is likely to be misdirected and could itself become a threat to freedom and to prosperity.

One of the themes is that the climate change movement has religious overtones which lead to intolerance and could, through inducing drastic centralised action, bring about restrictions on freedom. Sir Alan Peacock, in Chapter 6, for example, argues that the movement has the essential characteristics of a religion with its own prophets, its own sins against the environmental order and the possibility of atonement to provide salvation from those sins. The public statements of the Intergovernmental Panel on Climate Change (IPCC), he says, '... bear comparison with those of the prophets of old'; 'heretics' are identified and attempts are made to restrict their entry into the relevant professional debates; and there is only one route to salvation which must be taught in schools. Colin Robinson, in Chapter 3, also points to some of the religious aspects of the climate change movement, which he places in the context of apocalyptic predictions that foresee dreadful events, attribute them to sinful behaviour and then propose means of atonement. Russell Lewis, in Chapter 2, believes that environmentalism has turned into 'a kind of fundamentalist religion' which is a matter of faith and '… cannot be moved by argument or factual evidence'. He calls for a 'mood of honest scientific enquiry'.

Another theme is the need to have some historical perspective when assessing predictions of doom arising from damaging climate change. Russell Lewis provides numerous examples of 'global alarmism', going back to biblical times, resulting in predictions that have proved to be incorrect. Colin Robinson argues that apocalyptic forecasts belong to a class of prediction which emerges periodically as a consequence of uncertainty: it is easier to foresee problems, particularly those of the global variety, than solutions to those problems. There is a tendency to look to centralised action to deal with such issues, neglecting the revealed problems of central planning and the problem-solving capacities of markets which (as the history of events such as the 'energy crises' foreseen in the 1970s suggests) are powerful means of solving incipient problems.

As to the approach taken by governments, in Chapter 4 David Henderson argues that governments across the world are mishandling climate change issues. In part, this is a matter of the policies adopted to curb 'greenhouse gas' emissions. These too often take the form of costly regulation, rather than a general price-based incentive such as a carbon tax. More fundamentally, there is good reason to question the basis and rationale of policy. Too much trust is placed in the elaborate advisory process that governments have created, which finds its chief expression in the work of the IPCC. From the outset that process has been controlled by departments and agencies committed to the view that anthropogenic global warming is a serious threat. It has therefore been subject to a chronic bias that is shared by many outside commentators. In relation to climate change, there is a clear need to build up a sounder basis for reviewing the issues. Governments should ensure that they and their citizens are more fully and more objectively informed and advised.

Julian Morris, in Chapter 7, argues that the science of climate change is far from settled and that, though mild warming is a plausible outcome, it is reasonable to expect that new technologies will in the next fifty years result in 'dramatic reductions in greenhouse gas emissions as well as cost savings'. In his view, government attempts to reduce emissions drastically are likely to slow rates of economic growth, thus inflicting harm and reducing the capacity to adapt, particularly in low-income countries. He regards adaptation as the best strategy if there is a gradual warming trend and urges governments to remove barriers to adaptation, such as taxes and regulations, so that entrepreneurs can identify market niches and seek to fill them.

A very significant issue in climate change models is the rate of discount. These models usually look ahead many years (indeed, over two centuries in the case of the Stern Review) and they require a means of trading off present and future consumption levels. The rate of discount used in this trade-off is one of the major determinants of the results of the models. Sir Ian Byatt considers this issue in Chapter 5. It is sometimes assumed that very low rates of discount should be used out of concern for future generations, but Sir Ian argues it would be a major mistake 'to adopt such a low rate of discount that would put too many of our eggs into dealing with the future, leaving us impoverished today'. His contention is that using below-market, 'ethical' interest rates for projects designed to combat climate change would lead to severe dual-discounting problems and would result in extensive government intervention, blunting market incentives and producing unin-tended consequences. Like Sir Alan Peacock, he is concerned not only about the adverse impacts on living standards but the effect on freedom.

There is some agreement among the authors that, though drastic centralised action should be avoided, there is a case for making provision against the possibility of future damage from climate change. Both David Henderson and Ian Byatt favour the use of carbon taxes. Julian Morris thinks removal of barriers to adaptation is the principal appropriate policy response, though he sees virtue in a low rate of carbon tax as a means of promoting adjustment, perhaps using the proceeds to supplement private sector investment in research into geo-engineering in case 'more catastrophic warming' occurs. Colin Robinson argues that, to avoid overuse of the environment, there might appear to be a case for using 'market instruments' to set a price for carbon. He is doubtful about their use at present, however (because of likely government failure), and argues that successful adaptation through the market is likely, as it discovers means of avoiding adverse climate change and of adjusting to any effects that still occur.

In general, the authors of this volume take a far more sceptical view than is usual of the hypothesis that drastic action to combat severe climate change can be justified. They are far from being 'climate change deniers', but they are aware of the damage done by doom-mongering in the past, they perceive serious flaws in the processes that have led to consensus climate change forecasts and in the models that underlie those forecasts, and they see many scientific and economic uncertainties that justify their scepticism. Moreover, they are wary of the centralised action being urged by the climate change movement, which would be subject to the problems of central planning, would certainly have unintended consequences and, very significantly, would result in burgeoning government and severe restrictions on freedom. In their view, there is ample scope for adaptation through markets to any warming that occurs, though some of them believe there is a case for taxes on carbon or carbon trading in order to reinforce adaptive tendencies.

Such views are contrary to the conventional wisdom and will therefore be strongly resisted by the intellectual establishment that has invested heavily in the drastic climate change hypothesis and is trying to suppress dissent. But even the conventional wisdom of the day eventually breaks down when confronted by the 'march of events' and more powerful ideas.

References

Galbraith, J. K. (1958), *The Affluent Society*, New York: Mentor Books.

Hayek, F. A. (1949), 'The intellectuals and socialism', *University of Chicago Law Review*, Spring.

2 GLOBAL ALARMISM
Russell Lewis

Introduction

Being intellectually cool nowadays means trumpeting your belief that global warming will bring disaster to the human race unless radical action is taken. Various people are currently outbidding each other in warning of the wrath to come. Former prime minister Tony Blair (2004) has claimed that global warming is more of a danger than terrorism; government Chief Scientific Adviser Sir David King (2004) has implied that by the end of the century Antarctica will be the most habitable continent; the Archbishop of Canterbury, Rowan Williams (2006), foresees 'millions, billions' of deaths; and veteran environmentalist Sir James Lovelock, who regards our planet as a living creature – Gaia – asserts: 'we are now so abusing the Earth that it may rise and move back to the hot state it was in fifty-five million years ago, and if it does, most of us and our descendants will die' (Lovelock, 2006).

All very angst-making – were it not for the fact that we have heard it all before. Of course, there have been prophecies of doom since biblical times, but forecasts of ecological disaster are to be found more in the last two centuries. The Cassandra cries on assorted environmental pretexts have become deafening, however, only in the last fifty years or so. What they have in common is that, invariably, they have been false alarms.

The population growth false alarms

One very popular scenario among the doomsters has been that human population growth will outrun food supplies and result in mass starvation, unless enough people are previously removed by natural disaster, disease or war. It is an old theme put forward most persuasively by Thomas Malthus (Malthus, 1798). The crux of his argument was that human numbers will grow, like those of any other members of the animal kingdom, as long as there is enough food for them to survive, and then they will collapse when food runs out. Tragically, he claimed, while the human population grows geometrically, food supplies grow arithmetically. Starvation is therefore a perpetual threat to mankind, only to be avoided by sexual abstinence – forlorn hope!

Malthus certainly set the fashion of extrapolation: that is of assuming a constant percentage rate of growth of some form of human-related activity. It has been a prominent feature of apocalypse-mongering ever since. Famously, the American professor Paul Ehrlich latched on to it (Ehrlich, 1968), saying that the present doubling time for the world population was every 35 years. Thus in 900 years there would be 60 million billion people on earth. There is a major underlying fallacy here. This is the assumption that people merely respond instinctively and thoughtlessly to environmental conditions, like frogs, rats or pigeons. In fact the distinguishing characteristic of humans is that they are able to think, so they are able to adapt. One result of this ability to think and adapt is our technology. Instead of passively reacting to the environment we are able to change aspects of it. We do not automatically produce as many children as the food supply dictates. Contraception allows us to limit the number of children we have. Technological advance really does make all the difference. World population has about doubled in the last 50 years but the speed of microchips is doubling every eighteen months (Intel co-founder Gordon Moore's Law). Such considerations did not, however, give Ehrlich pause. Here are two of his more extreme pronouncements from the above book: 'The battle to feed humanity is over. In the 1970s and 1980s hundreds of millions of people will starve to death in spite of any crash programs embarked upon now. At this late date nothing can prevent a substantial increase in the world death rate ...'. He went on to predict the deaths of: 'A minimum of ten million people, most of them children, during each year of the 1970s. But this is a mere handful compared to the numbers that will be starving at the end of the century.'

Believing thus that doom was inevitable, Ehrlich felt that all he could suggest was a way of salvaging something from the wreck. He sought immediate action at home (in the USA) in the form of population control. He proposed taxes on children, giving 'responsibility prizes' to each couple for every five years of childless marriage, and to men who had vasectomies. If these failed it would be necessary to resort to compulsion. He advocated particularly ruthless policies towards underdeveloped countries, including the stoppage of all food aid to nations that experienced chronic food shortages. He reserved the harshest treatment of all for India, arguing for enforced sterilisation of all Indian men with three or more children.

The justification for such severity was: 'We already know that it is impossible to increase food production to cope with continued population growth. No improvement in underdeveloped countries' food production can do more than delay the day of reckoning unless population control is successful.'

The facts, however, have not been cooperative. 'Contrary to the predictions of many environmentalist ideologues, world food supplies have more than tripled in the last 30 years, staying well ahead of world population growth' (Borlaug, 2002). Fewer people are starving in the Third World and agricultural crops per person in developing countries have grown by 52 per cent. This is in part a product of the Green Revolution, which introduced higher-yield crops, but also owes much to irrigation and improved water control. The increased productivity has meant that more food could be produced from the same amount of land. Had global cereal yields of 1950 prevailed in 1999 then the world's farmers would have required nearly 1.8 billion hectares of land, instead of the 600 million that were used, to achieve the global harvest that was achieved in 1999.

Pessimists have suggested that the Green Revolution is over and that further improvements cannot be expected. On the contrary: 'Scientific breakthroughs, particularly in agricultural biotechnology will likely permit another 50 per cent increase in yields over the next 35 years if their development is not hindered by anti-science activism' (ibid.).

Meanwhile the price of food fell by more than two-thirds between 1957 and early 2001, making it much more available to the poor (Lomborg, 2001). Admittedly world grain prices have risen sharply of late, but this is partly at least caused by the US government's policy of heavily subsidising ethanol production (to reduce dependence on foreign oil), which has reduced the land available for growing cereals. Paradoxically, the rise in food prices has also been caused by the growing wealth, not the impoverishment, of large parts of the previously underdeveloped world.

In any case, the scary forecasts of huge and unmanageable

population growth have been made to look foolish. In the developed world, particularly in Europe, birth rates have fallen below the reproduction rate of 2.1. In the developing world too reproduction rates are falling, and the UN estimates that world population will stabilise around 2050.

Natural resources false alarms

Parallel to, and associated with, Ehrlich's dire prophecies of world overpopulation and starvation there have been dire predictions of scarcity of the energy, raw materials and other resources on which modern civilisation depends. Here too there was a repetition of a pattern set in an earlier period. In 1865 Stanley Jevons, a distinguished British economist, claimed in *The Coal Question* that Britain's industrial supremacy was destined to end because it was only a matter of time before the rising cost of mining coal at ever deeper levels would cripple the industries dependent on it. Worse still, he urged: '… it is useless to think of substituting any other kind of fuel for coal'.

He proved wrong about that, but soon, across the Atlantic, a series of eminent people were making similarly gloomy but much more strident and specific forecasts about oil, the fuel that was becoming just as vital to the American economy as coal was to Britain. In 1914, for instance, the United States Bureau of Mines predicted that American oil reserves would last ten years. Subsequently, in 1939 and in 1951, the Department of the Interior said American oil would last thirteen years (*The Economist*, 20 December 1997).

These scares, however, almost comically false as it turned out, were but curtain-raisers for what has become a canonical work for the environmental movement – the 1972 Club of Rome report on *Limits of Growth*. It used the newly fashionable techniques of systems analysis and computer simulation. For those who sought intellectual justification for their belief in approaching doom, this seemed to deliver the goods. Pointing out that total world oil reserves were 550 billion barrels, it asserted: 'We could use up all the proven reserves of oil in the entire world by the end of the next decade.'

Sure enough, 600 billion barrels were used up not in a decade but by 1990, so there should have been a deficit by then of 50 billion barrels. Yet at that date reserves had risen to 900 billion barrels. This howler of a prediction didn't stop the Club of Rome producing in 1992 *Beyond the Limits*, a revised edition of *Limits of Growth*, which predicted that the world would run out of oil in 2031 and gas in 2050. The above error about oil reserves keeps being made by people who should know better. Oil reserves are never remotely equivalent to all the oil in the earth's crust. The proven reserves are what the oil companies have decided to look for and which are known to be exploitable under prevailing technical and economic conditions. They are designed to provide the oil industry's working inventory of oil stocks. There is a limit to the amount of money the oil companies can spend on searching for more or deeper wells because prospecting and drilling are expensive, and there are other competing obligations which affect their long-term profits, such as advertising, marketing, research, building refineries and distribution. The best indicator of whether oil is getting scarcer is its price, and though prices have risen sharply in the last two years, that fact does not necessarily point to a long-term upward trend.

So what is the prospect for fossil fuel supplies? What one

can say is that there is little chance of them running out soon. The evidence is that there is enough oil in the ground (including conventional sources and unconventional sources, including oil shales, tar sands and coal bed methane) to last over two hundred years at the year 2000 rate of consumption. In addition there is enough natural gas for 500 years and coal for over a thousand years. Taking all fossil fuels combined, there is enough for 700 years of consumption at the year 2000 rates (Beckerman, 2003). The reserves may become more expensive to exploit but, at the same time, such costs will provide incentives for conservation, the development of alternative fuels and the development of new technologies.

The immediate concern about oil and gas supplies, which is engaging decision-makers in the West, is the large proportion of them in insecure places, namely the Middle East and Russia. That is why there is renewed interest in nuclear power, especially as it has the extra attraction for green-minded politicians that it produces no carbon dioxide emissions. Also, its radioactive emissions are lower than those from coal-fuelled plants. With the use of fast-breeder reactors it is estimated there is enough uranium available to keep nuclear power plants going for 14,000 years (Lomborg, 2001).

The Club of Rome forecast early exhaustion of other natural resources, including metals. Here its failure was even more dismal than in the case of fossil fuels, as shown by the following table setting out the growth of proven mineral resources.

Table 1 **Reserves and consumption of key minerals, 1970 and 1999**

	Estimated reserves (million metric tons)		Cumulative consumption (million metric tons, approx.)
Product	1970	mid-1999	1970–1999
Aluminium	1,170	34,000	430
Copper	308	650	290
Lead	91	140	150
Nickel	67	140	22
Zinc	123	430	190

Note: 1970 reserve estimates are from Meadows et al., 1972: 56–58. 1999 reserves estimates include 'demonstrated reserves that are currently economic or marginally economic plus some that are currently sub-economic' (*World Almanac* 2000: 31, taken from the U.S. Geological Survey and the U.S. Department of the Interior). The figures of aluminium reserves include bauxite expressed as aluminium equivalent. Consumption estimates are from *Materials Bulletin's Prices and Data,* annual (Surrey, UK: Metal Bulletin Books Ltd.).

Ecological false alarms
DDT

The most important, or at least the most influential, environmentalist book of the twentieth century was Rachel Carson's *Silent Spring* (1962). It was an attractively written all-out assault on pesticides, especially DDT. At the time it came out the general view was that nature was benign and that the main poisons found in the environment were synthetic toxins manufactured by man. We now know that the plant kingdom is teeming with toxins that plants have developed to protect themselves against predators. Carson took the view that DDT was the great threat to the environment and, eventually, it would build up in plants, animals and birds, working through the food chain, to the human race, to which it would prove fatal. Her evidence for this dismal prospect, however, was weak. She said that there were fewer birds because of the use of DDT in the previous twenty years. The American journalist Gregg Easterbrook made a scorecard of 40 birds that Carson said might now be extinct or nearly so (hence the title of her book). He found that nineteen were stable, fourteen increasing and seven in decline. That looked very much like business as usual (Easterbrook, 1995). Carson also referred to the Audubon Society's annual bird census as her source for reducing avian numbers, but those censuses actually showed their numbers increasing.

Her most alarming pronouncement, however, was that DDT was a poison staying put in the environment and gradually building up. This was refuted by Dr Philip Butler, director of the Fish and Wildlife Service's Sabine Island Research Laboratory, who found that '92 per cent of DDT and its metabolites disappear from the environment in 38 days' (US Environment Protection Agency's DDT hearings, p. 3726). He added that humans have no need to worry about small exposures to DDT. According to the World Health Organisation director in 1969:

> DDT is so safe that no symptoms have been observed
> among the 130,000 spraymen or the 535 million inhabitants
> of sprayed houses [over the past 29 years of its existence].
> No toxicity was observed in the wildlife of the countries
> participating in the malaria campaign. It has served at least
> 2 billion people in the world without costing a single human
> life.

The really scary claim in Carson's book was that DDT would cause 'practically 100 per cent of the human population to be wiped out from a cancer epidemic in one generation'. The theory was that a race of super-insects, impervious to pesticides, would emerge, threatening US farms. Desperate farmers would then triple the amount of pesticide they were using to combat the superbugs, destroying their crops. This would work up through the food chain, first killing the bugs, then the worms, then the birds, then the fish and finally the human race. This speculation was based solely on the fact that DDT spraying went on from 1940 to 1960 and that in that period cancer cases also increased. That is to say Carson assumed coincidence was causation. Yet the American Center for Disease Control, more plausibly, found a direct correlation between cancer rates rocketing and a surge in the use of tobacco. Other factors were sun exposure, obesity and lack of exercise. Also, as people were living longer, more of them contracted cancer because they had not previously died of something else.

Such errors might be forgivable but for their dreadful results. These results were the banning of DDT in the USA and the steering of international aid to prevent its use in the developing world. It is estimated that this removal of the most effective means of eliminating malaria has led to the deaths of 3 million people a year, most of them children and pregnant mothers, making a total of well over a hundred million (Sci Thread Archive, 2006).

Acid rain

The big environmental scare of the 1980s was the death of forests, said to be due to acid rain. The UN Brundtland Report stated flatly that 'in Europe, acid precipitation kills forests', and school textbooks on ecology today continue to repeat this charge. There was certainly evidence of sick and dying trees in the 1970s and 1980s in Europe: Bavaria in Germany was especially hard hit. In America the Blue Ridge Hills in North Carolina were severely affected. In some parts of them the sick-tree figure reached as much as 60 per cent. There were also claims that, owing to the same cause, many fish were dying in Swedish and American lakes. These alarms led to large-scale scientific investigation. The biggest one was the US National Acid Precipitation Assessment Program (NAPAP), costing $750 million. Its experiments showed that trees exposed to moderately acid rain, far from dying, actually grew faster. Its main conclusion was that 'the vast majority of forests in the US and Canada are not affected by decline ... Moreover there is no case of forest decline in which acidic deposition is known to be a predominant cause'. It also found that acid affected only 4 per cent of lakes and had only a very slight effect on buildings and monuments. In 1996 the annual report on the state of forests by the UN and the European Commission concluded that 'Only in a few cases has air pollution been identified as a cause of [forest] damage'. In the main, forest decline appeared to arise from local pollution, not acid rain, which of course is a cross-border phenomenon. One of the curiosities about the controversy on acid rain is that it proceeded 'in ignorance of the basic fact that rain is naturally acidic, but pundits declaimed an imminent doomsday for forests *at the very time when American forests were expanding*' (Easterbrook, 1995).

From global cooling to global warming

In the 1970s those who studied climate were much influenced by the experience of the previous 30 years of global cooling. There is a strong human tendency to believe that what has been happening in the recent past will continue to happen in the future. Sure enough, that decade was awash with forecasts of continued global cooling, while this was claimed to be a mere foretaste of the ultimate calamity – a new ice age. The intriguing thing is that some of the most prominent ice age doomsayers of the time included leading global warming enthusiasts of today. Notable among them were Sir Crispin Tickell (who later persuaded Margaret Thatcher to support the global warming thesis) in his *Climate Change and World Affairs* (see Lindzen, n.d.). A more spectacular change of direction came from Stephen Schneider, who, in recent times, has been described as a superstar of Greenhouse. In 1976, however, his book *The Genesis Strategy*, putting forward the forthcoming ice age thesis, was a best-seller. He had already set out his stall in a paper in 1971. This pinned responsibility for the prospective freeze-up on human activities, namely the discharge of aerosols into the atmosphere from power plants or domestic fires. In an interesting passage he discounted the countervailing effect of carbon dioxide, arguing that even an 800 per cent increase in CO_2 would give very little warming and would of itself raise temperature less than two degrees. In view of the fact that CO_2 has risen only 25 per cent since the Industrial Revolution, this would suggest that Schneider saw little potential in CO_2 at all, at least not in 1971. By the late 1980s, however, he had swung round to the UN view that a mere doubling of CO_2 would raise temperatures by 1.5 to 4 degrees, leading to a global warming catastrophe (www.johndaly.com/Schneider.htm).

Another ice age prophet of the 1970s was the journalist Lowell Ponte. His book *The Cooling* (a best-seller) followed the same line of reasoning as Schneider's, blaming humans for spewing particulates into the atmosphere in their reckless and wasteful use of energy, these particulates reflecting the sun's rays back into space, thereby reducing its warming effect and making the earth colder. It offered a stark future. As he said: 'The cooling has already killed hundreds of thousands of people in the poor nations … If it continues, and no strong measures are taken to deal with it, the cooling will cause world famine, world chaos, and probably world war, and this will all come by the year 2000.'

What were the strong measures the global coolers had in mind? Ponte suggested reviving an old Soviet plan, dating back to Lenin's time, to dam up the Bering Strait between Siberia and Alaska. A later Soviet version of it proposed installing giant atomic-powered pumps to suck up water from the Pacific Ocean's equivalent of the Gulf Stream, the Kuroshio Current, and pour warm water into the Arctic Ocean. Another scheme was to spray the Antarctic ice black, so that it would absorb instead of reflect the sun's rays and cause the ice to melt. Remembering some of the disasters brought about by Soviet engineers through diverting rivers – such as the one that emptied the Aral Sea – the imagination quails at the thought of what might have happened if the world's politicians had taken these half-baked plans as seriously as they currently treat measures to deal with the alleged global warming threat.

Conclusion

After surveying a series of eco-alarms over the last generation or so, *The Economist* (20 December 1997) concluded: 'Forecasts of scarcity and doom are not only invariably wrong, they think that being wrong proves them right.' It went on to chart the course followed by virtually every environmental scare story.

- Year 1: the scientist finds some potential threat.
- Year 2: the journalists amplify and exaggerate it.
- Year 3: the environmentalists join the bandwagon.
- Year 4: the bureaucrats move in; an international conference is demanded; regulations and targets proliferate.
- Year 5: a scapegoat, usually America (global warming), is sought out and denounced.
- Year 6: doubts surface among scientists.
- Year 7: the quiet climbdown: the official consensus estimate of the problem shrinks. The scare disappears not with a bang but with a whimper.

If this is the way the world works, so be it, but it does not have to be so. We can shrug our shoulders, but a real puzzle remains. Why is the present such an age of anxiety? The human race, as a whole, is healthier, better fed and housed, longer-lived and more prosperous than at any time in history. Children no longer die like flies. There is for most people far more security, leisure, culture and entertainment than ever before, and, contrary to the pessimists, who are always with us, the environment is vastly improved, especially in terms of clean air and water and surroundings in country and town. If there is anything dysfunctional about our civilisation, as Al Gore insists, it is that we are so blind to its benefits.

It is possible to accept aspects of the science of global warming without predicting a forthcoming apocalypse or highly coercive and centralising government action to deal with the consequences. The points raised in this chapter do not depend on whether a specific scientific theory of climate change is right or wrong: they are designed to illustrate that the consequences of environmental and ecological change are regularly exaggerated. But why do environmentalists cling so persistently on one pretext after another to the idea that climate change will be the precursor of forthcoming apocalypse? Michael Crichton believes that it is because environmentalism has become a kind of fundamentalist religion, which harks back to ancient myths deep rooted in the human psyche, such as Eden, the fall of man, the loss of grace and doomsday. As with other fundamentalist beliefs it is a matter of faith which cannot be moved by argument or factual evidence (Crichton, 2003). If this is so, these global environmental scares will recede only when environmental bigotry yields to honest scientific inquiry.

References

Beckerman, W. (2003), *A Poverty of Reason*, Independent Institute.

Blair, T. (2004), BBC News 24, 31 July.

Borlaug, N. E. (2002), *Global Warming and Other Myths*, Competitive Enterprise Institute.

Carson, R. (1962), *Silent Spring*, New York: Houghton Mifflin.

Crichton, M. (2003), 'Environmentalism as religion', speech to the Commonwealth Club, San Francisco, 15 September.

Easterbrook, G. (1995), *A Moment on Earth*, London: Penguin.

Ehrlich, P. (1968), *The Population Bomb*, New York: Ballantine Books.

King, Sir D. (2004), *Antarctica News Archives*, 4 May.

Lindzen, R. S. (n.d.), 'Global warming: the origin and nature of the alleged scientific consensus', www.eskimo.com.

Lomborg, B. (2001), *The Sceptical Environmentalist: Measuring the Real State of the World*, Cambridge: Cambridge University Press.

Lovelock, J. (2006), *The Revenge of Gaia*, London: Allen Lane.

Malthus, T. (1798), 'An essay on the principle of population'.

Meadows, Donella H., Dennis L. Meadows, Jorgen Randers and W. W. Behrens III (1972), *The Limits to Growth*, New York: Potomac Associates.

Sci Thread Archive (2006), 'Rachel Carson's ecological genocide', www.usenet.com, 8 May.

Williams, R. (2006), *Front Page*, 4 April.

3 CLIMATE CHANGE, CENTRALISED ACTION AND MARKETS[1]
Colin Robinson

The first part of this chapter considers the climate change issue by discussing the problems inherent in apocalyptic forecasting and the planning that normally accompanies it, contrasting them with the problem-solving capabilities of markets. It then moves on to some other issues of principle, particularly the weaknesses of climate change modelling. The third part examines the property rights question that underlies the climate change problem. The fourth part considers appropriate policy responses to present-day fears of climate change and its consequences. It abstracts from more detailed criticisms, made elsewhere (Carter et al., 2006; Byatt et al., 2006), of the Stern Review (Stern et al., 2006) and other recent analyses of the impact of climate change.

Apocalyptic predictions
A perspective

Apocalyptic forecasting, of which predictions of the dire consequences of climate change are one example, has a long history, which can be traced back at least to the Old Testament prophets (Robinson, 1972). The New Testament, of course, provides the

---

1   A fuller version of the arguments in this paper is in Colin Robinson, 'Economics, politics and climate change', Julian Hodge Lecture, Cardiff Business School, 2008.

somewhat more recent and more specific source document for the genre, in the Revelation of St John, chapter 6, where the four horsemen represent the forces of man's destruction and catastrophic events occur.[2]

Subsequent history is littered with forecasts that are recognisable as belonging to the same apocalyptic category in that dreadful events are foreseen unless people repent from some sin. As Sir Alan Peacock points out in his chapter in this volume, latter-day prophets of doom can be seen in a quasi-religious context in which they provoke feelings of guilt and then propose means of atonement. A characteristic sin is supposed lack of concern for future generations. So, for example, a recurring theme in the twentieth century was the claim that people were exploiting the earth's resources at a destructive rate which would leave insufficient for future generations: atonement was by acknowledging the error of their ways and adopting policies, such as reducing rates of depletion, which would leave more for their successors (see, for example, Robinson, 1975).

As each apocalyptic forecast emerges, there is a tendency to regard it as unique, with little recognition that it belongs to a general class of predictions. But the prevalence of such forecasts in the past suggests that, regardless of the precise nature of the expected source of doom, there are underlying reasons why, periodically, such forecasts emerge. Rather than being aberrations, they are evidently part of the normal course of events. The explanations are probably quite simple. First, as regards the supply side, the prophet of doom is a member of a profession that, as well as any money income it may earn, enjoys psychic income from the

---

2   Revelation, 6: 15, King James (Authorised) version.

effect of its prophecies on its audience: individual prophets may not be clothed in sackcloth and ashes but they enjoy supplying mental discomfort to their listeners or readers.

Second, and probably more important, the apocalyptic forecast is a natural reaction to the pervading state of uncertainty which creates both anxiety and a demand for predictions. At any point in time, any intelligent person can see numerous problems to which solutions have not yet appeared. That is so for the rather obvious reason that human ingenuity can, by definition, be directed at solving problems only after they have been perceived as such. Consequently, an abundance of unsolved problems is the norm. It is not difficult to find issues about which to be anxious – either that no solution is possible or that, if it is possible, it will not appear in time – particularly for people who have little sense of history. But the presence of unsolved problems is not, in itself, particular cause for concern. In the words of Dennis Gabor (1963), 'The problems of fifty years hence will not have to be solved by our present-day technology but by that which we shall possess in twenty or thirty years' time.'

Seen in this context, one way of regarding the apocalyptic forecast is as part of the process by which unsolved problems are indeed solved. By raising awareness of an issue, the forecaster sets in motion forces that produce solutions. On this view, the apocalyptic forecaster – whether St John or, at a lower level, Sir Nicholas (now Lord) Stern – is an unwitting part of the great machine that stimulates human ingenuity into producing the advances in knowledge and its application that deal with the problems that always confront us.

Forecasting and planning

There is, however, more to the apocalyptic forecast than that because it always contains a call to action. It comes in two parts. Part one is the 'conditional' forecast – what would happen on unchanged policy. Part two is the plan – what should be done to avoid the dire consequences that the forecast reveals. The latter-day apocalyptic forecaster, when turning to the plan, almost invariably recommends centralised solutions carried out by governments and international organisations. It would be unusual, if not unprecedented, for someone, having seen the apocalypse, to recommend leaving solution of the foreseen problems entirely to decentralised market forces. There must be coordinated, centralised national government or international action so that someone is seen to be doing something. Recommendations are usually for direct government intervention in the market by targets, regulations, government-controlled investment programmes, taxes or sometimes 'market instruments' (of which more later).

But there is a serious problem with the view that centralised action, via governments and international organisations, is required to avoid the apocalypse. This form of action suffers from the same inherent problems as does central planning, which has, wherever it has been tried, failed. Briefly, there are two reasons. First, the information required for centralised action to work – which is information about the future – cannot readily be gathered. Information is not available off the shelf, to be collected together in Whitehall or similar locations, because it is essentially decentralised and much of it is tacit. The production and dissemination of information are primarily market phenomena and the suppression of markets, which is the inevitable consequence of central planning, also suppresses the information that planners would need if they were to operate successfully.

The second problem is that, even if the information were available, the incentives to deal with problems are lacking. There is no Whitehall counterpart to the powerful self-interest motives to solve problems that exist in markets. On the contrary, the pursuit of self-interest by people in organisations that have a monopoly of policy-making is most unlikely to be to the public benefit. Public choice theory has shown the dangers of assuming, as much mainstream economic theory does, that politicians and bureaucrats, domestic and international, are wise, far-sighted and disinterested and will simply identify and then pursue the 'public good'.

Markets as adaptive systems

By contrast, the market system is essentially a massive problem-solving mechanism. Markets may appear to operate slowly and 'imperfectly' but they do so surely: their existence is the reason why past apocalyptic forecasts have not come true. Competitive markets are powerful adaptive systems which contain strong incentives to solve the problems of the day, whether trivial or apparently serious. Unfortunately, the essence of the market's functions is often clouded by the mechanistic neoclassical models used by many economists which concentrate on end-states of markets rather than the processes by which they adjust to change.

Hayek's insight – that competition is a process of discovery, quite different from stylised textbook models of competition which show the states of markets once competition has been exhausted – is the key to understanding the problem-solving power of markets (Hayek, 1948). Competitive markets provide the information and the incentives that spark the discovery process in which human ingenuity is exercised to deal with economic, social and technological problems. Marketplace incentives, operating mainly through price signals, induce entrepreneurs to seek out and then exploit market opportunities so as to make profits. Sometimes, entrepreneurial action may result in no more than the discovery of a slightly cheaper way of making a product or a slightly more efficient method of organising a firm. At other times, it may result in a major invention and its subsequent exploitation with global consequences. On a Hayekian view, the apocalyptic forecaster/ planner who believes he or she can see a long way into the future and has the answer to the world's problems, substituting for and surpassing the problem-solving capabilities of markets, has been misled into the 'pretence of knowledge', if not into a 'fatal conceit' (Hayek and Bartley, 1988).

Of course, no one can be sure that there will always be an economic or technological fix for every conceivable problem that ever arises. But past history, including the failure of predicted catastrophes to materialise, suggests that market systems act effectively to deal even with predicted global disasters. Russell Lewis's chapter in this volume gives some examples of past false predictions of catastrophe. One particularly apposite example, on which it is worth dwelling because it is the most recent and the one that bears similarities to the concerns of today, is the 'energy crisis' of the 1970s when there was a consensus that rapid depletion of energy resources (especially crude oil), allied with the exploitation of monopoly power by the Organisation of Petroleum Exporting Countries (OPEC), would result in ever-rising energy prices. 'The days of cheap energy are gone for ever' was the slogan of many commentators, unwise enough to think they could see 'for ever' into the future. Only centralised action by governments and international bodies could, it was argued, avoid a major world energy crisis. In the event, despite the almost total absence of the government and international action that had been deemed so important, energy markets adjusted to the 'crisis' so that, within ten years, the world was (by the mid-1980s) awash with oil and OPEC was meeting to try to prop up crude oil prices. Instead of crude oil prices tripling in real terms by the end of the century, as had been the consensus of forecasts in 1980, they began to decline almost as soon as the forecasts were made and halved by the end of the century. Even in the first half of 2008, despite increases in crude prices in the previous few years, they were still lower in real terms than in 1980.[3]

Climate change and its consequences

History shows that concerns about resource exhaustion and monopolisation of energy sources appear periodically: there are some signs that the concerns of 30 years ago are beginning to resurface. But the most likely source of the apocalypse is now perceived to be climate change, which receives constant media attention, as did its predecessor, the 'energy crisis' of the 1970s. In fact, climate change fears were a subplot in the 1970s 'crisis', when there was a consensus among climate scientists which was the opposite of today's: global cooling was the perceived threat, as an article in *Newsweek* at the time made clear.

> The central fact is that after three quarters of a century of extraordinarily mild conditions, the earth's climate seems

---

3   BP's Annual Statistical Review of Energy shows a series of crude oil prices back to the early days of oil exploration and discovery in the second half of the nineteenth century.

> to be cooling down … Climatologists are pessimistic that
> political leaders will take any action to compensate for the
> climatic change, or even to allay its effects. They concede
> that some of the more spectacular solutions proposed such
> as melting the arctic ice cap by covering it with black soot …
> might create problems far greater than those they solve.[4]

It should be a matter of concern to those who now claim that 'the science is settled' that the opposite view was generally held only 30 years ago. Nevertheless, present-day forecasts of the dire consequences of warming cannot be dismissed simply on the grounds of this fundamental change in the consensus in a relatively short time.

The usual hypothesis about climate change is that emissions of carbon dioxide and other 'greenhouse gases', from the use of energy and from other human activities, will lead to a future trend towards warming of the earth and consequential damage to economic and social life. The following are the principal links in the chain that can lead to conclusions about prospective climate change and its effects.

A climate change trend?

Since the climate is always changing, the damaging-change hypothesis is difficult to pin down, but those who support it must think there is a warming *trend*. If we were merely in the upward phase of a *cycle*, caused by natural forces, presumably there would be much less cause for concern because, by definition, the direction of the cycle would reverse and global warming would be replaced

---

4   *Newsweek*, 28 April 1975. I am indebted to Julian Morris, who pointed out this
    article to me.

by global cooling. Determining whether warming is a trend or just part of a cycle is extremely difficult, given the apparent very long timescale of climatic change, yet, from a policy point of view, the distinction between trend and cycle is clearly vital: if warming is to be replaced by cooling in the relatively near future, as part of the same natural cycle, action now to curb warming might well have perverse effects. The amplitude and length of any cycle are also critical issues.

The link with greenhouse gases

There is scientific evidence that, other things being equal, increasing emissions of carbon dioxide and other greenhouse gases will bring rising world temperatures. In the absence of complete scientific knowledge, however, the list of the 'other things' and their effects is long but incomplete. Most climate scientists would, like most economists, readily admit that their models are gross simplifications and that large areas of ignorance remain. Working out what happens when other things are constant is therefore not easy and it seems that experience in the twentieth century must lead to some doubts about the exact causal link between emissions and warming: despite continuously rising emissions during the century, the warming occurred in two periods (1920–40 and 1975–98), with slight cooling in between the two periods and no clear trend in the last ten years or so.

Economic and social consequences

Even if it could be established that there is a clear warming trend caused by greenhouse gas emissions, there are still important questions to be answered about the extent to which this trend will be damaging and also about the extent to which natural adaptation will deal with any economic and social consequences. If it seems that action to combat the trend should be taken, the issue then arises of what form it might take and what the costs might be compared with the benefits.

Bearing in mind the issues just set out, some matters of principle that underlie current predictions of climate change and its consequences, particularly those in the Stern Review, are discussed below.

Long-term predictions

The Stern Review, like other attempts to predict climate change and its consequences, attempts to look a very long way ahead – up to two centuries. Consequently, the validity of its results depends principally on whether it is possible, given our present state of knowledge, to draw useful conclusions from analyses by climate scientists, economists and other social scientists, to integrate them and to project them into the far distant future in a way that provides an adequate basis for policy in the sense that one can have confidence that both the future direction of change and its approximate magnitude are correctly predicted. If the direction of change is incorrectly predicted, policies intended to offset the change will be perverse: presumably today's scientists would think that the policies suggested in the *Newsweek* article quoted above would have been perverse because they would have been based on the assumption that the world is cooling. Less seriously, if the direction of change is correctly predicted but the magnitude is significantly in error, policy will not be proportionate to the problems that emerge.

Some reasons to doubt whether we can have such confidence are explained below, together with some comments on the robustness of Stern's policy conclusions.

Uncertainty about the science

The treatment of scientific evidence in the Stern Review has been criticised elsewhere (Carter et al., 2006). It seems to attach remarkably little uncertainty to the estimates of climate change and its impact that it uses. Indeed, the following passage suggests that the authors think that, in the case of the scientific evidence, it is risk (outcomes have known probability distributions) rather than uncertainty (outcomes have unknown probability distributions) which is relevant:

> ... scientists are now able to attach probabilities to the temperature outcomes and impacts on the natural environment associated with different levels of stabilisation of greenhouse gases in the atmosphere. Scientists also now understand much more about the potential for dynamic feedbacks that have, in previous times of climate change, strongly amplified the underlying physical processes. (Stern et al., 2006: iii)

If the assumption is that the science is now so well defined that the relevant probability distributions are known into the far distant future, that would be a remarkable conclusion.

Modelling and uncertainty

At the root of the Stern Review and similar attempts to forecast climate change and its effects are its modelling efforts, though

Stern also attempts some more disaggregated and qualitative analysis. Different time horizons are used in different places but they are all very distant. The review explains, 'The analysis of climate change requires, by its nature, that we look out over 50, 100, 200 years and more' (ibid.: x).

It is in its use of very long-term predictions that the 'pretence of knowledge' aspect of the review is most obvious. Quite properly, in various places, the review expresses due caution about interpreting the results of modelling so far ahead, which requires 'caution and humility', though by the time conclusions are drawn such reservations seem to fade.

It is often supposed to be virtuous to look ahead for long periods. Both markets and governments are sometimes criticised because they have short time horizons and do not pay sufficient regard to the interests of future generations (their implicit discount rates are too high). But there are good reasons why individuals and organisations do not habitually peer many years into the future and act on what they think they see. It is because, in practice, it is not possible to see far into the future and make enough sense of it to act usefully on the results. Inability, not unwillingness, to look into the far distant future is the issue. Consequently people and organisations take limited views of the future, taking what action they can to anticipate future events but also adapting as they go along, using rules of thumb and other simple decision rules to muddle through in the presence of uncertainty. With decentralised decision-making in markets, there are many views of the future and the forecasting problem is 'solved' imperfectly through different forecasts, rules of thumb and adaptation.

In the climate change case, the danger is that, given our very limited ability to foresee changes in climate, technology, the economy and society, long-term views are more misleading than helpful. Human myopia cannot be overcome simply by well-meaning attempts to build models that purport to peer decades and centuries ahead. Action taken now, in anticipation of supposed long-run trends, may concentrate on the wrong issues and make matters worse rather than better. Centralised action, which constitutes a large part of Stern's recommendations, risks major mistakes. Such action, by governments or international organisations, concentrates on consensus views (which have frequently been wrong in the past), creating information monopolies and suppressing dissenting opinions, as David Henderson points out in another chapter in this volume.

In addition to the time horizon, there are problems related to the modelling in the review. Modelling is a valuable tool in economics because it forces the conceptual structures of models and their parameters to be made clear. Moreover, in principle it permits learning from experience in the sense that a post-mortem on a forecast (which, except by chance, will be incorrect) will reveal whether structure or assumptions were at fault (Robinson, 1970).

But when the system that is being modelled is poorly understood and predictions over a very long period ahead are being made, there is a clear danger that formal modelling will be more misleading than helpful. In the climate change case, the Stern Review uses some models that purport to 'integrate' climate models with models of economic and social linkages to climate change. Integrating two poorly understood systems, and making projections that go far beyond the range of previous experience, moves the 'forecast' into unknown territory, surrounding it with massive uncertainty. Moreover, the danger is that, because the models appear to be able to quantify the future, the results will be given far more weight than is their due. In Chapter 6, Part II of the Stern Review, where these modelling exercises are discussed, the uncertainties that surround their results are discussed. But caution seems to evaporate as the review goes on. Towards the end we can observe examples of a common phenomenon against which forecasters have to try to guard – that, because of the amount of effort they have put into their predictions, they begin to believe in their own results, no matter how shaky the foundations. Hence, on page 450 we read: 'This Review has made a compelling case for action – on both mitigation and adaptation – demonstrating that the global economic costs of business as usual paths are likely to far outweigh the costs of taking action to reduce the risks.'

And, by page 572, there are 'clear and strong conclusions' about the dangers of government inaction which could lead to '… risks of major disruption to economic and social activity, on a scale similar to those associated with the great wars and the economic depression of the first half of the 20th century'.

It is simply implausible to believe that the models that Stern uses can reveal sufficient about the future for any reasonable person to draw such firm conclusions. Because they relate to systems about which there is considerable ignorance, and because they go so far ahead, it seems most unwise to suggest that they can indicate so certain a long-term future.

Markets and global environmental problems

Heroic attempts to quantify changes in climate and their effects centuries ahead give a false impression that such quantification can be helpful and suggest that the outlook is more certain than it is. Nevertheless, one should beware of jumping from the deficiencies of the Stern Review and its ilk to the conclusion that future climate change is not and cannot be a problem. It is conceivable that man-made climate change is occurring and that in the future it will cause difficulties unless preparations are made to offset its effects. That is a separate issue that ought to be examined.

Differences in principle between resource depletion and global environmental issues

In principle, there are reasons why global environmental problems might be more difficult to solve via markets than the apparent resource depletion problems that have in the past caused alarm but which markets have dealt with so adequately. A significant difference in the case of resource depletion is that there are price signals that encourage changes in the depletion rate in the 'right' direction, as indeed they did at the time of the 'energy crisis' in the 1970s and 1980s. For reasons discussed by Harold Hotelling (1931) in a seminal paper in the 1930s, changes in price expectations and discount rates tend to determine depletion rates (assuming technology and resource deposits to be given). For example, if there is a perception of increasing scarcity of a resource, future prices are expected to be higher relative to costs than previously anticipated, and there are two effects that increase the life of remaining resources. First, resource owners cut current production, holding back resources to reap the higher profits they expect from selling at increased future prices: as they reduce supply, current prices increase. Second, this increase in current prices induces consumers to reduce their demand. It was such effects which turned the oil 'scarcity' of the 1970s into the oil 'surplus' of the

1980s. But these benign market effects depend on the presence of appropriate market institutions, and in particular on there being clearly defined and enforced property rights.

Property rights and market 'failure'

Provided property rights are clear and are enforced by government, as they are or can be for many environmental assets, owners will defend their rights against potential polluters, as they would against other intruders, and markets will work reasonably well. But where property rights do not exist or are difficult to establish, as in the case of the global environment, use of the environment will be free as far as a polluter is concerned, so there will be an external cost that is not fully taken into account by the market and there will be a tendency to overuse the environment as a sink for wastes. The natural environment has public good characteristics in that people cannot be excluded from using it and no charge can be made for that use. For such reasons, the Stern report describes climate change as the result of the 'greatest market failure of all time'. Consequently, there appears to be a case for collective action (including national government and international action) to avoid overuse of the environment.

The policy response
Picking winners

One policy response would be direct action by governments to promote energy sources and technologies that reduce carbon emissions compared with the present. The two main candidates are nuclear fission power and renewable forms of energy, such as wind, solar, wave and hydro power. Many governments in developed countries have in recent years been wary of permitting nuclear investment, partly because of the long history of over-optimistic costs forecasts for nuclear power (Robinson and Marshall, 2006), but principally because of the potential adverse effects associated with nuclear fuel use and storage that have made nuclear power unpopular with electorates. In the face of climate change fears, however, there are signs of a revival of interest in nuclear generation.

Renewable sources are already being favoured by governments. The British government, for example, is providing large subsidies for wind power in the hope of reaching a target of 10 per cent of electricity generated from renewables by 2010, with an 'aspiration' to reach 20 per cent by 2020.[5] The European Union is setting even more ambitious targets that would involve member states increasing the share of renewables in their energy (not electricity) supplies to 20 per cent by 2020. Another form of direct government action, but on the demand rather than the supply side, is to try to persuade consumers to use less energy by subsidising home insulation and other means of 'conservation'. All manner of restrictions on people's freedom to choose fuels and technologies are now being imposed, with five-year 'carbon budgets' in the background (under a proposed new Climate Change Act), in an attempt to influence consumers to change their ways in directions that governments think desirable.

The problem with direct promotional action by government

---

5   These various targets and measures to try to achieve them are set out in DTI, *Our Energy Future – Creating a Low Carbon Economy*, Cm. 5761, 2003; DTI, *The Energy Challenge*, July 2006; and Department for Business, Enterprise and Regulatory Reform, *Energy White Paper*, May 2007. See also David Simpson, 'The economics and politics of wind power', in Robinson (2006).

is that it does not address the basic property rights issue that is at the root of the apparent climate change problem. Instead, it involves government in the difficult process of 'picking winners', whether that 'winner' is nuclear power, some form of renewable energy, 'clean coal' technology or energy conservation. Past attempts at picking winners have been notoriously unsuccessful (e.g. Myddelton, 2007), not just because of specific failings of particular ministers but for much deeper reasons of principle involving inherent information failures and the influence of pressure groups.

Most analyses of climate change policy are silent on these issues of principle. The Stern Review, for example, ignores completely the economic analysis of government action, exemplified in the 'public choice' theory that has been brought to such prominence by James Buchanan, Gordon Tullock and others,[6] and the Hayekian view of competitive markets.

The Hayekian critique of government action, as explained earlier, emphasises the role of markets as discovery processes that produce information and embody powerful incentives to solve incipient problems which governments cannot match. It is complemented by the public choice critique, which suggests that the chances are low that governments will improve welfare by attempts to pick winners. Governments are not disinterested servants of the public good: they are, for example, susceptible to the influence of pressure groups (unmentioned and apparently unrecognised in the Stern Review), which are likely to be very influential in pushing their own interests when governments are known to be searching for technologies to support. As explained

6   As Sir Alan Peacock points out (1992), the public choice approach has its roots in the work of David Hume and Adam Smith.

earlier, governments face the most serious problem of central planners – that they cannot gather the information they need, which is essentially decentralised and would have been produced by markets had it not been suppressed by government intervention. Into the vacuum come pressure groups that supply information that supports their causes. 'Blinding with science' is a common approach by pressure groups faced by governments short of the relevant knowledge on which to judge their proposals.

Using 'market' instruments

Direct action by governments is part of the Stern prescription. If we rule it out, for the reasons just suggested, we are left with an approach that is more appealing to most economists. That is to apply standard microeconomic theory by introducing some general economic instrument that will take into account the externality and will then allow the market to adjust without being constrained by the views of the government about which energy sources are most acceptable and how much energy should be conserved (Marshall, 2005).

One such instrument would be a 'carbon tax' – a tax on fuel that varies according to the carbon emissions produced when the fuel is burned. Since the optimal tax cannot be calculated, the tax rate would have to be determined by government and so government failure would be involved in applying the economic principle. Another instrument, instead of directly putting a price on carbon by applying a tax, is a carbon trading scheme under which permits to emit specified amounts of carbon are allocated and trading of those permits encourages efficiency in reducing emissions; such a scheme would allow a price of carbon to emerge.

Carbon trading is favoured in the Stern Review and there were experiments with such schemes before one was introduced by the European Union in January 2005 (Nicholson, 2005).

A case for collective action?

To summarise, there is a theoretical case for collective action (which could include action by governments and international organisations or voluntary collective action) where there appear to be particularly damaging environmental effects from energy production, distribution and use that cannot be reduced by the allocation of property rights. Anthropogenic global climate change may be an example. We do not know whether it will occur and, if it does, whether it will be damaging. But, to guard against possible damaging climate change, we could take counteraction by pricing carbon, either by taxing it or by establishing carbon trading schemes.

At this point, mainstream economic theory has no more to say. But we should be wary of stopping analysis at this point. The views of economists who make the case for 'market instruments' are understandable, particularly if their case is that, once such instruments are established, no further intervention in the market should be required. Nevertheless, we should recognise that there is an element of misrepresentation in the term 'market' instrument. Carbon taxes and carbon trading could just as well be labelled 'interventionist' instruments. In one case, the government sets a price and lets the quantity of carbon adjust; in the other case, it sets a quantity and lets the price of carbon adjust. There is less potential for failure than in picking winners regarding specific technologies or consumption patterns that might reduce carbon use but failure is still probable. Whether it is setting prices or quantities, a government is acting in ignorance of what the price or the quantity 'should' be, and so we cannot be confident that its actions will be welfare-improving. Indeed, the one example we have of a major carbon trading scheme – the European Emissions Trading Scheme – is not encouraging since it has been subject to such severe government failure that it may now be difficult to rescue it from the discredit in which it stands. The initial setting and the subsequent resetting of the level of permits and their allocation have caused serious problems.

One serious, if neglected, question is whether, even if there is genuine evidence of damaging climate change, governments can be trusted to act effectively when applying either market instruments or other policies. Will they, for instance, give priority to *appearing* to be doing something, as they did in the energy 'crises' of the 1970s? There is a great deal of political posturing going on at present about climate change policy. In the EU, for example, summits and other gatherings result in grand declarations about targets for big cuts in future carbon emissions in the rather distant future. Nevertheless, at the same time, member country leaders are undermining the targets they set collectively by lobbying to make sure that their countries, or industries within their countries, are treated as 'special cases' that do not have to meet the targets. The case for collective action hinges on the idea that, in the absence of clear property rights, the market will not work well because there will be numerous freeriders. But most EU governments are at present trying to obtain a free ride by letting their fellow member states bear the costs of any carbon reductions. The same is true of the numerous international gatherings where politicians consider successors to the Kyoto agreement.

Political leaders clearly want to gather the electoral benefits of being seen to be 'green' without actually imposing on their electorates the costs of doing so. It is tempting to set very long-term targets – such as reducing greenhouse gas emissions by 60 per cent by 2050 (or possibly 80 per cent, as some would like), supported by five-year carbon reduction targets, as the British government has done. But these targets go far beyond any horizon in which present-day politicians are interested and should be treated with great suspicion. In general, if there is to be an improvement in the market outcome resulting from government action, the government in question needs to be far-sighted, wise and able to identify the 'public interest' and willing to pursue it. It is not, I think, unduly cynical to question whether either governments in representative political systems or international bureaucracies have such characteristics: certainly that is the conclusion of public choice economics.

Can markets deal with the climate change problem?

By contrast, well-functioning markets with appropriate institutions tend to produce benign reactions to emerging problems. Even though the vast majority of intellectuals think only of centralised action, there are great benefits in reliance on market responses, which permit gradual and flexible adjustment to perceived problems, which tend to act in the right direction (if not always as quickly as idealists might wish) and which avoid the restrictions on freedom which are one of the principal external costs of government action. These market responses are genuine 'automatic stabilisers' which work whether central authorities will them to or not.

Even apparently massive problems – such as those foreseen in energy markets in the 1970s and early 1980s – tend to yield to market forces. Most mainstream economists assume that appropriate market institutions do not exist in the climate change case because of the property rights problem mentioned earlier, but that view can be challenged. Even in cases where goods appear to be 'public', it may be that the degree of 'publicness' is exaggerated.[7]

If there is general concern that the natural environment is becoming overused, the effect may be *as if* it were owned. Actions by individuals are characterised not so much by narrow self-interest (in the self-centred sense) but by broader interests that include concern for family, friends and descendants. Let us assume that a large part of the population is very concerned about the world in which their children and grandchildren will grow up. In such circumstances, one would expect that both consumers and producers (the latter both spontaneously and as a reaction to the views of consumers) would act in ways they perceive would protect their successors. If, rightly or wrongly, a significant part of the population is concerned that there will be damaging climate change in the future unless something is done, it will demand and will be supplied with goods and services that are deemed 'green' (in the sense of reducing greenhouse emissions). Market forces could thus tend to correct an emerging climate change problem. The 'perpetual referendum' that constitutes the market – which means that people are voting every day by expressing their preferences – will produce votes for 'green' outcomes which producers, in their own self-interest, 'not from benevolence' (Smith, 1776: Bk 1, ch. 11), will satisfy.

---

7   Energy security is a case in point. See Robinson (2007).

Already such reactions are widespread. Much marketing now revolves around green claims. Many suppliers of goods and services say they are reducing their 'carbon footprints'. No doubt some claims are false and others are exaggerated. Nevertheless, actions to mitigate climate change and its effects are now regarded as potentially profitable. Consequently, a market reaction in favour of 'green' goods and services is under way. It may be 'imperfect' and halting but, if you regard the pursuit of profit as a more certain mechanism for getting things done than action through the political process, this market reaction is to be welcomed. Decentralised action appears already to be stimulating the discovery both of means of making adverse climate change less likely and of means of adapting to any change that still occurs, promoting the necessary technology and associated investments. As indicated earlier, some benign effects may stem from forecasts of adverse climate change, provided they are not exaggerated, because they stimulate such decentralised action through markets.

Of course, would-be centralisers, including most of those who carry out research in the climate change field, do not like the idea that market forces could be left to cope with the climate change 'problem'. Like all pressure groups, they would like to see their own views implemented through the medium of government. They characterise the market forces route as a 'do-nothing' approach. It is certainly not that. It relies on the reactions of millions of people and it is perfectly possible that decentralised market forces, resulting from the expression of people's preferences, are capable of overcoming the major obstacle to adjustment away from any global environmental issues that may be emerging – the absence of property rights in that global environment (the global commons problem). The absence of an owner of the global environment will cease to be a serious problem if a large body of people in effect become substitute owners and therefore guardians of the natural environment. It is rational for people to contribute towards the provision of a 'public good', even though they are supporting freeriders, if they believe it will otherwise not be provided (de Jasay, 1994).

The apocalypse and practical policy

Once the apocalyptic forecast is seen in context and the likely failures of government action are recognised, the case for urgent, centralised action against climate change seems much less convincing than the conventional wisdom of the day would have it. Most likely, now – as in the past – many analysts have become carried away by the results of their models, which purport to look into a far distant future, and have convinced themselves that they must embark on a crusade to enlighten others. Dissent must be discouraged and, in a mild version of the Inquisition, the views of anyone who questions the conventional wisdom should be disregarded and, if possible, suppressed.

On a cooler view of climate change, a more constructive approach would be to recognise the huge uncertainties that exist and to seek flexible means of dealing with the problems that may arise. Direct promotion by governments of particular ways of 'solving' the perceived problems is unlikely to succeed and is only too likely to have unfortunate side effects, including constraints on individual freedom. Market instruments, such as carbon trading systems or carbon taxes, are preferable to direct government action, but it is doubtful whether they can be justified at present when we can see a spontaneous market reaction in favour of 'green' products and services. The call for centralised action is much more about the appearance of being busy than about useful action against climate change. It runs the risks of major errors, even in the direction of policy.

A big advantage of relying on markets is their flexibility and adaptability. Views about global warming will change. We should beware of assuming that the prevailing scientific consensus will persist. In the future, warming may appear a more serious issue than now, in which case markets will enhance the profitability of 'greenery', so reacting in the 'right' direction. Or it may seem less serious, so that 'greenery' starts to go out of fashion and the market again reacts in the right direction. Can we be so confident that the big programmes now being urged by the climate change alarmists would show a similar degree of adaptability to changing circumstances? They are all too likely to set communities on courses that are very difficult to alter as the views of climate scientists change.

References

Byatt, I. et al. (2006), 'Economic aspects', in 'The Stern Review: a dual critique', *World Economics*, October–December.

Carter, R. M. et al. (2006), 'The science', in 'The Stern Review: a dual critique', *World Economics*, October–December.

de Jasay, A. (1994), 'Public goods theory', in P. J. Boettke (ed.), *The Elgar Companion to Austrian Economics*, Cheltenham: Edward Elgar.

Gabor, D. (1963), *Inventing the Future*, London: Secker and Warburg.

Hayek, F. A. (1948), 'The meaning of competition', in *Individualism and Economic Order*, London: Routledge.

Hayek, F. A. and W. W. Bartley (1988), *The Fatal Conceit*, Chicago, IL: University of Chicago Press.

Hotelling, H. (1931), 'The economics of exhaustible resources', *Journal of Political Economy*, 39(2).

Marshall, E. C. (2005), 'Energy regulation and competition after the White Paper', in C. Robinson (ed.), *Governments, Competition and Utility Regulation*, Cheltenham: Edward Elgar.

Myddelton, D. (2007), *They Meant Well . . .*, Hobart Paper 160, London: Institute of Economic Affairs.

Nicholson, C. C. (2005), 'Emissions trading: a market instrument for our times', in C. Robinson (ed.), *Governments, Competition and Utility Regulation*, Cheltenham: Edward Elgar.

Peacock, Sir A. (1992), *Public Choice in Analytical and Historical Perspective*, Cambridge: Cambridge University Press.

Robinson, C. (1970), *Business Forecasting: An Economic Approach*, Nelson.

Robinson, C. (1972), *The Technology of Forecasting or the Forecasting of Technology*, Surrey Papers in Economics.

Robinson, C. (1975), 'The depletion of energy resources', in D. W. Pearce (ed.), *The Economics of Natural Resource Depletion*, London: Macmillan.

Robinson, C. (ed.) (2006), *Regulating Utilities and Promoting Competition*, Cheltenham: Edward Elgar.

Robinson, C. (2007), 'The economics of energy security: is import dependence a problem?', *Competition and Regulation in Network Industries*, 8(4).

Robinson, C. and E. Marshall (2006), 'Can a new nuclear programme be justified', *Economic Affairs*, June.

Smith, A. (1776), *Inquiry into the Nature and Causes of the Wealth of Nations*.

Stern, N. et al. (2006), *Stern Review: The Economics of Climate Change*, London: HM Treasury.

4 GOVERNMENTS AND CLIMATE CHANGE ISSUES: QUESTIONING A CONSENSUS[1]
David Henderson

I believe that governments across the world are mishandling climate change issues. In this chapter I shall consider, first, the forms that this mishandling has taken, and second, very briefly, a possible route to improving matters. By way of setting the scene, I will begin by outlining the present situation and events leading up to it.

An official worldwide consensus

In relation to climate change issues, there exists a worldwide and well-established official consensus. With few exceptions, governments are firmly committed to the view that anthropogenic global warming constitutes a serious problem which requires official action at both national and international level. A recent high-level restatement of this consensus position is contained in the Declaration issued at the close of the G8 Summit meeting in Heiligendamm in June 2007. In paragraph 49 of the Declaration the G8 leaders said that 'global greenhouse emissions must stop rising, followed by substantial global emission reductions'. They

---

1   This chapter formed the basis for a presentation in Vienna on 8 October 2007, under the auspices of the Hayek Institut. At various points it draws, without specific attribution, on a paper of mine which was published in *World Economics*, 8(2), April/June 2007.

thus reaffirmed the case for what are often described as 'mitigation' policies.

In pretty well every democratic country, this official consensus is not at all a matter of political controversy: to the contrary, it enjoys general cross-party support. Indeed, in the world as a whole I can think of only one political leader who is a convinced and open dissenter, namely the president of the Czech Republic, Vaclav Klaus. Governments generally, and opposition parties too where they exist, have determined that policies designed to curb emissions are called for, and that the existing array of policies needs to be extended and reinforced.

This official multi-partisan consensus is not new. Climate change issues, and in particular the extent and possible consequences of anthropogenic global warming, have been on the international agenda for twenty years or more; and it is now over fifteen years since governments decided, collectively and overwhelmingly, that determined measures should be taken to deal with what they agreed was a major problem. The decisive collective commitment was made in 1992, through the United Nations Framework Convention on Climate Change (UNFCCC), which almost all countries have ratified. The Convention specifies that its 'ultimate objective' is: 'to achieve … stabilization of greenhouse gas emissions in the atmosphere at a level that would prevent dangerous anthropogenic interference with the climate system'. Precisely this form of words is repeated in the Heiligendamm G8 Summit Declaration.

Since 1992, many governments have acted, at state and provincial as well as national level, and collectively within the European Union, through what is now a wide range of measures and programmes, to curb emissions of (so-called) 'greenhouse gases'. On the international scene, through the Kyoto Protocol, 'Annex I' countries have undertaken to meet specific targets for emissions reductions. It is true that these Kyoto-based commitments are viewed by many as relatively unambitious, or as a first step only, and that in almost all the countries concerned they seem unlikely to be met. But the accepted direction of policy remains clear and unquestioned; and both nationally and internationally new and far-reaching measures to curb emissions are under consideration or in prospect.

In taking this line, governments have met with widespread and increasing public approval. Prominent among the unofficial sources of support are media commentators on environmental and scientific issues, scientific bodies, environmental NGOs and, increasingly, large business enterprises. Let me add that there is widespread support for the official consensus position among economists, as evidenced, for example, in the Stern Review (2006) on *The Economics of Climate Change* and some of the reactions to it. As usual, however, our profession is not of one mind.

The basis for consensus

What was it that persuaded governments, fifteen or more years ago, to take the possible dangers of anthropogenic global warming so seriously, and what is it that has caused them to maintain and even intensify their concern? I think the answer is straightforward. From the start the main influence was, as it still is, *the scientific advice provided to them*. That advice can and does come from many sources; but the main single channel for it, indeed the only channel of advice for governments *collectively*, has been the series of massive Assessment Reports produced by the Intergovernmental Panel on Climate Change, the IPCC.

The IPCC was established by governments in 1988, as the joint subsidiary of two UN agencies, the World Meteorological Organisation (WMO) and the United Nations Environment Programme (UNEP). Its first Assessment Report, which appeared in 1990, formed a basis and point of departure for the negotiations that led up to the drafting of the Framework Convention. Since then, the Panel has published three further such reports. The latest of these, referred to for short as AR4, was completed and published in the course of 2007. As with earlier reports, it chiefly comprises the separate volumes produced by each of the Panel's three Working Groups. Between them these volumes come to nearly 3,000 pages, and some 2,500 experts – authors, contributors and reviewers – were directly involved in preparing them: I refer to this small army of participants as the IPCC *expert network*. AR4 was finally rounded off with an overall Synthesis Report.

The IPCC does not itself undertake or commission research: the Assessment Reports review and draw on the already published work of others. Most of this work is financed by governments, and these governments thus have their own direct sources of information and advice: their thinking and actions do not necessarily depend on what the Assessment Reports have said. All the same, the IPCC's work continues to carry substantial weight, with public opinion as well as the Panel's member governments, because of its wide-ranging coverage, its extensive and ordered participation, and the fact that it alone is designed to serve the world as a whole.

These IPCC reports are unique in their scope. They deal with the whole range of issues relating to climate change, including economic as well as scientific and technical aspects. In producing them, the Panel has brought together teams of specialists drawn from across the world, and put in place ordered procedures for directing and reviewing their work and arriving at agreed final texts. It has secured for the reports and their conclusions the acceptance of its many and diverse member governments; and in consequence, it has helped to guide the thinking of those governments.

An explicit tribute to the work of the Panel is paid in the G8 Summit Declaration: 'Taking into account the scientific knowledge as represented in the recent IPCC reports, global greenhouse emissions must stop rising, followed by substantial global emission reductions.'

More recently the work of the Panel has received further and conspicuous international recognition through the award of the 2007 Nobel Peace Prize, which it shared with Al Gore. The citation for the award says that the Panel 'has created an ever-broader informed consensus about the connection between human activities and global warming'; and actually this form of words does not do justice to the full range of topics that the IPCC covers.

On the basis of the three Assessment Reports that have been prepared since the Framework Convention was signed, governments have certainly no reason to question the position that they adopted more than fifteen years ago. To the contrary, these reports have served to confirm and strengthen that position.

So much for the official and widely accepted consensus and its basis. Given this background, you might well ask, how it is that I, an economist and not a scientist, have come to question the considered stance that so many governments have continued to take, chiefly on the basis of the scientific advice they have been given and with substantial and increasing public support. What justification do I have for taking the line that governments across the world are mishandling climate change issues?

Aspects of mishandling: the content of policies

My concerns fall under two headings: first, the *basis and rationale* for current policies, the thinking that enters into them; and second, their actual *content*, the measures and programmes that governments have adopted. My main emphasis here is on the former aspect, but before turning to it I would like to make a general point about actual mitigation policies.

Many economists – for once, there may even be a consensus – hold the view, which I share, that policies to curb CO_2 emissions should principally take the form of economy-wide price-based incentives, through a carbon tax or auctioned tradable permits, rather than administrative measures. This is the position taken, for example, in a recent official report from the Productivity Commission in Australia. The report argues that the core of policy should be 'a national emissions price signal', whether through an emissions trading scheme or a carbon tax, and that, if such a signal 'can do the heavy lifting, other directly substitutable measures should be discontinued ...'

Although price-based mitigation measures, chiefly through emissions trading schemes, currently operate in many countries (and in some subsidiary jurisdictions too), they are far from providing 'heavy lifting'. For one thing, the trading schemes have not involved full auctioning of permits, so that they have been administered rather than (or as well as) price-based measures. For another, most of the measures taken have not been price based. Everywhere, mitigation policies chiefly comprise a long and growing list of regulatory initiatives – specific grants, subsidies and tax remissions; specific mandatory targets, as for renewable energy and biofuel use; detailed specifications for vehicles, buildings and equipment; and town planning directives. Such initiatives have been justly described by Martin Wolf, in his *Financial Times* column of 16 March 2007, as 'a host of interventionist gimmickry'.

These wide-ranging interventionist packages give rise to obvious dangers.

- First, they may pay little regard to the cost-effectiveness of the measures concerned, so that emissions reductions are made costlier than they would be if the same results were secured through 'uniform prices': a range of different implicit carbon prices is created.
- Second, they create an array of opportunities for lobbying and rent-seeking – as also do emissions trading schemes, as currently operated.
- Third, they involve, and open up the further probability of, a range of worrying intrusions on the freedom of people and enterprises.

In this latter context, the American commentator Paul Driessen has with good reason made the point that such developments: '... would change life as we know it. They would give alarmist politicians, bureaucrats and activists a leading role in every housing, cooling, transportation, manufacturing, agricultural, business and consumer decision'.

Foreshadowing doom

The risks of intrusive and even coercive action are heightened by the alarm-prone treatment of climate change issues which now prevails in many countries, not least my own. It is widely taken as established beyond question that humankind is placing the planet under dire threat, that further drastic measures of mitigation are urgently required, and that such measures should extend to the conduct of individual, family and business life through explicit and detailed codes of behaviour.

Here are some summit-level instances of what I call the heightened milieu consensus. They go beyond the sober language of the G8 Summit Declaration:

- Tony Blair, then still prime minister of the UK, commenting in October 2006 on the Stern Review on the economics of climate change, said that 'what is not in doubt is that the scientific evidence of global warming caused by greenhouse gas emissions is now overwhelming ... [and] ... that if the science is right, the consequences for our planet are literally disastrous'.
- Blair and the Dutch prime minister, in a joint letter of October 2006 to other EU leaders, wrote that 'We have a window of only 10–15 years to take the steps we need to avoid crossing a catastrophic tipping point'.
- Stephen Harper, prime minister of Canada, in a speech in 2007, described 'climate change' as 'perhaps the biggest threat to confront the future of humanity today'.
- President Sarkozy of France, in some remarks in May 2007 on climate change policies, said: 'We know now that we are the last generation that can prevent catastrophe'.

Such assertions are not directly drawn from the IPCC Assessment Reports. They are bold extrapolations from the reports, with a clear presumptive element. They are, however, in tune with much public thinking, and they are presumably sanctioned by the scientific advisers and environmental departments concerned.

These quotations have brought me to my central and final theme, which is the beliefs, perceptions and presumptions that underlie the current policy consensus. This brings me back to the IPCC. Not all of those who subscribe to the consensus would go so far as the political leaders that I have just quoted; but all of them, like the G8 Summit leaders, can point to a large body of scientific argument and opinion, and in particular to the IPCC and its series of reports. The Assessment Reports are seen as giving expression to a worldwide scientific consensus, based on an informed and objective professional evaluation, and therefore providing a sound basis for policy. Let me explain why I have come to question this picture.[2]

Questioning the IPCC process

Why do governments, and outsiders too, place so much trust in the IPCC's role and work? I think that the trust largely results from the wide and structured expert participation that the IPCC process ensures. People visualise an array of technically competent persons whose knowledge and wisdom are effectively brought to bear through an independent, objective and thoroughly professional scientific inquiry. Indeed, many observers identify the Panel with the network, as though well-qualified and disinterested

---

2   The IPCC's role and work form the subject of a group of articles, including an important contribution by David Holland, in a recent issue of *Energy and Environment*, 18(7/8). The authors include John Zillman, who was a leading participant in the IPCC's work from the earliest stages; and his article offers a much more favourable assessment of the IPCC process than mine.

experts were the only people involved.[3] The reality is both more complex and less reassuring.

There is a basic distinction that has to be made between the IPCC itself and the IPCC *process*. The process involves three quite distinct groups of participants. First, there is the *Panel* itself, which controls the preparation of the reports. It effectively comprises those officials whom governments choose to send to Panel meetings. Generally speaking, these are not high-ranking persons. They include both scientists and laymen. Numbers are not fixed, but a typical Panel meeting might involve some three hundred designated participants. Working directly for the Panel is the IPCC *Secretariat*, though this is a small group whose functions are mainly of a routine administrative kind. A more influential body is the 28-strong IPCC *Bureau*, comprising high-level experts in various disciplines from across the world, chosen by the Panel. The Bureau acts in a managing and coordinating role under the Panel's broad direction.

Second, there is the 2,500-strong expert network, which, however, is quite distinct from the Panel itself. There is little or no overlap between the two bodies.

Last but far from least, there are the government departments and agencies that the Panel reports to: it is here, and not in the Panel itself, that the ultimate 'policymakers' are to be found. The relevant political leaders and senior officials within these departments and agencies make up what I call the *environmental policy milieu*. In addition, leading members of the IPCC Bureau, past

---

3   Among leading scientists, one example is the professor at Yale University who has (wrongly) described the IPCC as 'a respected international group of hundreds of scientists' and as 'comprised of scientists from 99 countries' (Ehrlich, 2005: 138, 169).

as well as current, can also be classed as members of this policy milieu; and together with the most influential members of the Panel, these persons make up what may be termed the informal *directing circle* of the IPCC.

Policy commitment

Now while the IPCC as such has been formally instructed by governments that its reports 'should be neutral with respect to policy', this instruction must be intended to refer specifically and exclusively to the contribution made by the expert network through the reporting process. The official Panel members, together with the policy milieu that they report to, are almost without exception far from neutral: they are committed, *inevitably and rightly*, to the objective of curbing emissions, as a means to combating climate change, which their governments agreed on when they ratified the Framework Convention; and in many cases they are likewise committed to the kinds of policies that their governments have adopted in pursuit of that objective. As officials, they are bound by what their governments have decided. This is the context within which the three successive IPCC Assessment Reports prepared since 1992 have been put together in the network and reviewed by member governments. The clients and patrons of the expert network, with few exceptions, take it as given that anthropogenic global warming is a serious problem which demands, and has rightly been accorded, both national and international action.

Not surprisingly, this working assumption is shared by leading officials in the international policy milieu. Here, among many cases that could be cited, are three recent examples. They are public statements made in February 2007, following the publication of the report of Working Group I, which forms the first volume of AR4:

- Dr Pachauri, the chairman of the IPCC, and hence of the IPCC Bureau: 'I hope this report will shock people [and] governments into taking more serious action';
- Achim Steiner, the Director-General of the UNEP: 'in the light of the report's findings, it would be "irresponsible" to resist or seek to delay actions on mandatory emissions cuts';[4]
- Yvo de Boer, Executive Secretary of the Framework Convention: 'the findings leave no doubt as to the dangers that mankind is facing and must be acted on without delay'.

These are strong assertions, like those that I quoted earlier from political leaders. In none of them was the wording taken directly from the report in question: these eminent persons were going beyond the text, to draw their own confident and unqualified personal conclusions as to the lessons for policy. While they were fully entitled to form and air these opinions, their statements were not just summaries of 'the science', nor of course were they 'policy neutral'.

It is against this background, of a policy milieu that is not and cannot be neutral, and in which leading figures are convinced that anthropogenic global warming is placing the world under imminent threat, that some basic features of the expert reporting process have to be borne in mind:

---

4   This and the following quotation are taken from a report (3 February 2007) in the *Financial Times*.

- the choice of lead authors for the Assessment Reports largely rests with the already committed member governments, since lists that they provide form the starting point for the selection process;
- complete draft texts of the working group reports go to these governments for review; and
- it is governments, as represented in the Panel, which sign off the final versions of the Assessment Reports and amend the draft Summaries for Policymakers before they approve these also for publication.

The fact is that departments and agencies that are not – and cannot be – uncommitted in relation to climate change issues are deeply involved, from start to finish, in the preparation of the Assessment Reports.

Errors, omissions and bias

Does this fact put in doubt the expert reporting process? I would say: 'no, not necessarily'. I have come to believe, however, that the reporting process is in fact badly flawed, in ways that reflect a built-in high-level official bias. Despite the numbers of persons involved, and the lengthy formal review procedures, the preparation of the IPCC Assessment Reports is far from being a model of rigour, inclusiveness and impartiality.

In some areas, the expert process has not ensured appropriately broad professional involvement. A case in point is the treatment of statistical issues. A leading American statistician, Edward Wegman, has noted that:

> The atmospheric science community, while heavily using statistical methods, is remarkably disconnected from the mainstream community of statisticians in a way, for example, that is not true of the medical and pharmaceutical communities.

As for economics, Ross McKitrick, in written evidence to the House of Lords Select Committee on Economic Affairs, argued that after the Second Assessment Report, which appeared in 1995, 'the IPCC could no longer claim to have the participation of mainstream professional economists'. I think that the subsequent list of AR4 participants lends support to this view.[5]

The treatment of economic issues within the IPCC process has been subject to justified criticism. In particular, a weakness in some IPCC documents has been the use of invalid cross-country comparisons of output (real GDP), based on exchange rates rather than purchasing power parities. Just as measures of output over time within a country or currency area have to correct for *changes* in the price level, so cross-country measures of real GDP need to correct for price *differences*; and this is done through purchasing power parity converters. Since exchange-rate-based comparisons do not allow for cross-country price differences, they give a distorted picture of the world economy and the course of change within it.[6]

---

5   Professor Wegman's observation was made in one of his responses to questions put to him in the course of an inquiry carried out by a committee of the US House of Representatives. McKitrick's evidence to the Select Committee is on pp. 262–3 of Vol. II of the Committee's report, which appeared in 2005.

6   From late 2002 on, Ian Castles and I jointly put forward a critique of some leading aspects of the IPCC's economic work, while authors involved in that work contested our criticisms: these exchanges were published in the journal *Energy and Environment*. I reviewed and carried farther the whole debate in a later article in the same journal (16(3/4), 2005), which among other things sets out the rationale of purchasing power parity converters.

A basic general weakness is the uncritical reliance on peer review as a qualifying criterion for published work to be taken into account in the assessments. Peer review provides no safeguard against dubious assumptions, arguments and conclusions if the peers are largely drawn from the same restricted professional milieu. What is more, the peer review process as such may be insufficiently rigorous. This can be a serious concern when what is in question is the derivation and processing of large data sets. Peer review does not guarantee due disclosure of sources, methods and procedures so that results can be replicated by others.

Failures of disclosure, such as many journals would not tolerate and which would not be permitted in business prospectuses, have characterised published work that the IPCC has drawn on. The most notable case is that of the temperature reconstructions which entered into what became known as the 'hockey-stick' study. This piece of work, which was prominently featured and drawn on in the Panel's Third Assessment Report and afterwards, formed the basis for a memorable and widely accepted claim that in the northern hemisphere the 1990s had been the warmest decade of the millennium, and 1998 the warmest single year. Probably no single piece of alleged evidence relating to climate change has been so frequently cited and influential. The authors concerned failed (and later declined, until eventually strong pressures were brought to bear) to make due disclosure, and neither the publishing journals nor the IPCC required them to do so. Similar problems have also arisen in relation to instrument-based temperature series of which the IPCC reports have made use.

The handling of the disclosure issue by what I call the IPCC's directing circle reflects no credit on those involved: they have failed to acknowledge the problem and take appropriate action. In the relevant sections of AR4 the issue is simply evaded. In relation to this and other questionable features of the reporting process, the response of the IPCC milieu to informed criticism has typically been inadequate or dismissive.[7]

I have now come to think – and the thought was not in my mind when I first became involved with climate change issues, more by accident than design, five years ago – that the IPCC process, viewed as a whole, is not professionally up to the mark. I think that the main reason for this chronic deficiency is a strong and continuing element of bias that has always entered into it, a bias that goes beyond the simple commitment of the official participants to what their governments have decided.

From the earliest days, most if not all of those directing the process have shared the conviction that anthropogenic global warming presents a threat, to humanity and the planet, which demands prompt and far-reaching action by governments; and had this not been the case, and known to be the case, *they would not have attained their leading positions within it*. To take only the three current examples just quoted: Pachauri, Steiner and de Boer would not have sought their respective posts, nor would they have been seen by UN agencies and member governments as eligible to hold them, had they not been identified as fully committed to 'consensus' views. The same has been true throughout of the Bureau and other leading figures. The IPCC process is run today, as it has been from the start, by true believers.

---

7   The issues covered in these last few paragraphs – of non-disclosure, non-response, selective coverage and bias within the reporting process – are treated at length in an important article by David Holland (Holland, 2007) and more recently by R. McKitrick (McKitrick, 2008).

The salvationist context

Some history is relevant here. Within the environmental policy milieu, there is a generic bias that goes a long way back and extends well beyond issues relating to climate change. Members of the milieu, together with their outside allies and supporters, have typically embraced the beliefs and presumptions that make up what I have termed *global salvationism*.[8]

In the salvationist picture of the world, two elements are combined. One is an unrelentingly sombre picture of recent trends, the present state of the world (or 'the planet'), and prospects for the future unless governments involve themselves more closely, and with immediate effect, in the management and control of events. Within this picture, environmental issues are treated almost exclusively in terms of problems, dangers and potential or even imminent disasters, with the presumed harmful effects of economic growth on current lines as one reason for concern. The second element is a conviction that known effective remedies exist for the various ills and threats thus identified: 'solutions' are at hand, given wise collective resolves and prompt action by governments and 'the international community'. The global salvationist thus combines dark visions and alarming diagnoses with confidently radical collectivist prescriptions for the world.

Against this background, the issue of global warming, and the dangers that it might present, came as a new and powerful reinforcing element to an already established framework of thought. In pointing to new threats and new 'solutions', it has served to confirm and extend already established salvationist convictions.

Of course, this historical link with questionable salvationist

---

8   The content, history and implications of global salvationism form the main theme of ch. 4 of Henderson (2004).

beliefs can be seen as no more than coincidental: in itself, such an association does not put in doubt the findings of climate scientists or the competence and objectivity of the IPCC expert network and the reporting process. It is possible to accept the present official consensus on climate change issues, and the IPCC's latest Summaries for Policymakers, without signing up to the distorted picture of the world given in Agenda 21 and its successors. Indeed, it is not difficult to find strong critics of global salvationist pessimism who nonetheless accept that anthropogenic global warming is both real and a cause for concern: a prominent example is Bjørn Lomborg (2001). The close relationship between the IPCC milieu and its sponsoring departments and agencies, however, together with the already ingrained salvationist propensities of both, have, I think, from the start, and increasingly over time, put in question the objectivity of the IPCC process and hence its claims to authority. The professional advice that governments continue to rely on has been, and still is, suffused with bias.

This bias, and the convictions that it reflects, explains the readiness of the IPCC directing circle to make strong public pronouncements of the kind I have quoted, which go beyond the more restrained and qualified language of the Assessment Reports; to turn an unseeing eye to the disclosure failures and other defects in the reporting process; and to view with equanimity or approval the chronic lack of balance that characterises public debate on climate change issues. These propensities form the background against which the flaws in the expert reporting process have to be seen.

Summing up

In relation to climate change issues, governments have locked themselves into a set of procedures, and an associated way of thinking – in short, a *framework* – which both reflects and yields over-presumptive conclusions biased towards alarm. These conclusions form the basis both of current policies, which incidentally raise problems of their own, and of proposals to take those policies farther. They go beyond the bounds of professional consensus; they take as their prime source the results of a flawed process; and they represent a dubious extension of those results.

Even if the IPCC process were beyond challenge, it is imprudent for governments to place such heavy reliance, in matters of extraordinary complexity where huge uncertainties remain, on this particular source of information, analysis and advice. In fact, the process is flawed, and this puts in doubt the accepted basis of the established official consensus.

In relation to climate change, there is a clear present need to build up a sounder basis for reviewing and assessing the issues. Governments should ensure that they and their citizens are more fully and more objectively informed and advised.

What can be done?

In considering how the present situation might be improved, the main focus has to be on governments. It is they that fund major programmes and decide policies, while only they can reform the process that they have created and over which they have full control. In that connection, let me put just one central argument and point to its implications.

My argument is this. So long as the handling of climate change issues is left almost entirely to environmental departments and agencies there is little or no prospect of reform. A necessary condition for change, albeit not a sufficient condition, is that other departments of state should become effectively involved.

In particular, since the economic stakes could be high, a responsibility here rests on the economic departments of state – treasuries, ministries of finance and economics, and, in the USA, the Council of Economic Advisers. I am myself a former Treasury official; and much later, as a member of the OECD Secretariat, I had close dealings with economics and finance ministries in OECD member countries. I have been surprised by the failure of these ministries to get to grips with climate change issues, their uncritical acceptance of the results of a process of inquiry that is so obviously biased and flawed, and their lack of attention to the criticisms of that process which have been voiced by independent outsiders – criticisms which, I think, they ought to have been making themselves.

Such a conclusion points to official action on four related fronts.

- First, governments could improve the advisory process in general, and in particular the IPCC process within it, by making it more professionally watertight. For a start, they should insist on true and full disclosure as a precondition for published work to be taken into account in the review process.
- Second, they should no longer presume or aim at consensus. Rather, they should see to it that, both within the IPCC reporting process and more broadly, serious differences of professional opinion are aired.

- Third, they should consider developing sources of information and advice that are independent of the IPCC process, thus bringing to an end the Panel's virtual monopoly status as a source of collective advice.
- Fourth, they should broaden the basis of official participation, so that it goes beyond the existing well-entrenched environmental policy milieu.

Not all of these lines of action require international agreement: much could be done by individual governments acting on their own account. If even one or two influential governments were to question their current presumptions, and act accordingly, this could change the whole situation.

Postscript

Since the above text was prepared, both the OECD and the IMF have become more closely involved with climate change issues, in conjunction with finance and economics ministries within their member countries. This broader official involvement could have led to a more informed and less presumptive treatment of the issues. There is as yet, however, no sign that the opportunity will be recognised as such, while recent published work by the IMF is seriously flawed (see Henderson, 2007 and 2008).

References

Ehrlich, R. (2005), *Eight Preposterous Propositions: From the Genetics of Homosexuality to the Benefits of Global Warming*, Princeton, NJ: Princeton University Press.

Henderson, D. (2004), *The Role of Business in the Modern World*, London: Institute of Economic Affairs.

Henderson, D. (2005), 'SRES. IPCC and the treatment of economic issues', *Energy and Environment*, 16(3/4).

Henderson, D. (2007), 'New light or fixed presumptions? The OECD, the IMF and the treatment of climate change issues', *World Economics*, 8(4), October/December.

Henderson, D. (2008), 'Over-presumption and myopia: the IMF on climate change issues', *World Economics*, 9(2).

Holland, D. (2007), 'Bias and concealment in the IPCC process: the "hockey-stick" affair and its implications', *Energy and Environment*, 18(7/8).

Intergovernmental Panel on Climate Change (2007), *Climate Change 2007*, Cambridge University Press.

Lomborg, B. (2001), *The Sceptical Environmentalist: Measuring the Real State of the World*, Cambridge: Cambridge University Press.

McKitrick, R. (2008), 'Response to Henderson article', in *The Global Warming Debate*, published by the American Institute of Economic Research.

Stern, N. et al. (2006), *Stern Review: The Economics of Climate Change*, London: HM Treasury.

Zillman, J. (2007), 'Some observations on the IPCC assessment process 1988–2007', *Energy and Environment*, 18(7/8).

5 WEIGHING THE PRESENT AGAINST THE FUTURE: THE CHOICE, AND USE, OF RATES OF DISCOUNT IN THE ANALYSIS OF CLIMATE CHANGE[1]

Ian Byatt

In this chapter I cover four issues: first, the use of discount rates in the Stern Review which exaggerate the costs that may be associated with emissions of greenhouse gases; second, the distortions attendant on the use of discount rates that are well below those observed in markets; third, the massive difference made to any estimates of the costs of global warming by using market rates rather than those used in the Stern Review; and, finally, the problems of dual discounting that confuse the analysis of policies both to mitigate and to adapt to emissions.

The issues and the options
Estimates of damage

The conclusion of the Stern Review, that the damage resulting from not acting now substantially to reduce emissions of greenhouse gases greatly exceeds the costs of mitigation, depends crucially on its use of very low discount rates based on social time preference theory.[2] While there are many other areas of conten-

1   I am grateful for helpful comments from Partha Dasgupta, David Henderson, William Nordhaus, David Simpson, Andrew Tyrie, Martin Weitzman and two anonymous referees.
2   Since writing this chapter, Lord Stern's Ely lecture to the American Economic Association has been published (*American Economic Review: Papers & Proceedings*,

tion, the use of higher, and more defensible, discount rates based on market observations would overturn the key conclusion of the Review, namely that drastic and immediate action is required to avoid a situation comparable to two world wars and the interwar economic depression.[3]

The costs of not acting are said to be at least 5 per cent of GDP and possibly as much as 20 per cent of GDP, 'now and for ever'. 'Now and for ever' is, however, simply a expression for the present value of costs, many of which are forecast to occur in the 22nd century, discounted at a very low rate, probably the 1.4 per cent it used for long-term analyses. The use of higher discount rates would reduce these costs very substantially.

Potential distortion of investment to the detriment of future living standards

Discount rates also act to influence investment decisions in the market economy. These discount rates typically include allowance for the risks and uncertainties involved in specific cases. Any discount rates used in analyses of climate change should be properly related to wider decisions in the market economy, where costs are incurred now in order to achieve benefits in the future. Such investment is not only a matter of expenditure, but involves anything, such as a tax or restriction on the use of goods

---

2008, 98:2, 1–37). In this lecture, he appears to have adjusted his position and now talks of 'an SDR (Social Discount Rate) of 1.5–5%' (p. 17). This is a wide range, not fully covered in the simulations in the Stern Review, and, moreover, covering very different pointers to action, ranging from the immediate and drastic action advocated in the Review to a much more measured response.

3   For the other many points of contention, see, e.g., 'The Stern Review: a dual critique', *World Economics*, 7(4): 165–232.

and services, that involves incurring a cost now, which should lead to a benefit in the future, in the form of a greater abundance, or better quality, of goods and services, i.e. of things that make people better off.

To be worthwhile, a prospective investment should earn a return that is at least at least as good as the return that would have been earned on investments that might be displaced, or, in the jargon of economists, it should cover its opportunity costs. Otherwise it would risk making an inferior use of scarce resources and so reducing living standards compared to what they might have been.

While climate change may sometimes lead, for example, to exacerbation of disease and crop failure, there are many other ways to deal with such issues and their costs need to be balanced against the costs of reducing emissions. While climate change may, in some cases, make us less well off, any crowding out of investment in other activities – which predominantly take place indoors – occurring as a result of mitigation policies, will also reduce both our potential living standards and the available stock of physical and human capital, compared with what would otherwise have prevailed.

Differences in rates used

A mainstream approach in economics argues that the discount rate used in investment appraisal should be the reciprocal of the return earned on physical and human capital – some 5 to 6 per cent a year, and possibly more, in real terms, i.e. after allowing for the effect of inflation. These returns allow for project risk and for uncertainty. The Stern Review is an outlier, recommending the use of much lower discount rates – 2.1 per cent a year for this century and 1.4 per cent a year for the longer term. Evidence presented later in this chapter indicates the dramatic importance of discount rates in the estimates of costs made by the Stern team and by others.

The Stern Review argues for the use of low discount rates on grounds of 'social time preference' rather than basing the argument on the level of returns on capital. This approach abstracts from uncertainty. It makes a virtue of arguing that ethical judgements about future generations should be imposed from above. In these ways it advocates living in a different world from the market economy that has served us well, economically and politically, for the last 250 years.

Where there is dispute on numbers as important as these, sensitivity analysis is essential. Yet none was undertaken until a technical appendix to a postscript appeared. This showed that an increase in the discount rate from 1.4 per cent to only 3.5 per cent would reduce the estimates of the economic cost of greenhouse gas emissions from 5 per cent to 1.4 per cent of GDP. A wider range of sensitivities is essential to better public understanding of the issues.

Are we – or is the market – myopic?

The view that we mortal humans do not pay enough attention to the needs of future generations is a familiar one. It was raised by David Hume in the pre-industrial age and still resonates today. Some argue, for example, that private saving is insufficient to provide decent pensions (e.g. Munnell and Sass, 2008). But looking at individual savings, and individual myopia, is only part of the story. There are collective processes, working both through the market economy and through government, that are important determinants of the final outcomes for both investment and savings. Governments spend money on facilities such as hospitals, schools and roads. And in the market economy, we have developed a set of processes that have provided us with results that have given us, and promise to continue to give us, rates of economic growth that are unprecedented in human history. Their continuation would provide amply for future generations.

They involve innovation, the testing of innovations in methods of production and new products in competitive markets, within a framework of physical and human infrastructure, law and good civil government. They have raised living standards in market economies by some 2 to 3 per cent a year – and more during periods of catch-up, raising living standards by more than sevenfold over a period of 100 years – linked to a dramatic increase in life expectancy. The Industrial Revolution may have brought us carbon emissions, but it also brought hugely better living standards for vast numbers of poor and undernourished people – a process that is still under way.

High levels of investment and saving in both the private and public sectors have been boosted by international as well as national factors. Nineteenth-century Britain exported savings on a massive scale. Currently, savings in China and Japan are fuelling investment in the USA. But although this process may appear robust, history has shown that it can be checked, by bad policy or by damage to international trade. Already there are worrying arguments for tariff barriers against goods from countries said not to be doing enough to reduce CO_2 emissions.

'Dual discounting' and policies for mitigation and adaptation

There is a wide range of policy options, ranging from technological improvements in existing processes to massive reliance on renewables, for mitigating, or adapting to, emissions of greenhouse gases. Remedies advocated also include a host of ad hoc interventions, such as the phasing out of incandescent light bulbs and insistence on 'carbon neutrality' for new housing. Resources are already being spent on a considerable scale, for example on wind turbines.

The Stern Review confuses analysis of these matters by raising the spectre of 'dual discounting'. If all potential investment projects were to be appraised at the discount rates advocated by the Stern Review, there would be a massive increase in the number and scale of apparently viable projects in both the private and public sectors. This would be unmanageable; some method of discrimination would be required. The Review fails to face up to this. Are different discount rates to be used for different projects? Should projects to mitigate climate change, for example, be appraised at lower discount rates than other activities in the economy, including activities that will enable us to adapt to climate change?

Unless there are clear criteria, there is a risk of damage to the market economy by crowding out investment that would otherwise raise our living standards and increase the stock of capital to deal with events in the future. There is also risk of comprehensive government intervention in the decisions of individuals and companies, involving high costs, blunting incentives, damaging market processes and generating a series of unintended consequences with adverse effects on living standards – and on political and economic freedom.

The use of discount rates based on the return to capital, however, would enable policies to mitigate climate change, and to adapt to it, to be incorporated into the workings of a market economy. They could, for example, as suggested by William Nordhaus, be approached in a gradualist way by starting with a relatively low carbon tax. The level of such a tax could, as suggested by Ross McKitrick, be linked to measured temperature levels.[4]

The underlying analysis
The need for discounting

Policies designed either to abate the speed of climate change, or to adapt to its consequences, involve changing the time pattern of the use of goods and services, typically advancing expenditure by diverting it from other uses, to increase income or wealth in the future.[5] When examining these trade-offs, discount rates are used to weight the economic value of the resources used at different points in time. Because they refer to the valuation of costs and benefits, not to money, they should be in 'real' terms, i.e. adjusted to remove the effect of inflation.

Social time preference theory

The Stern Review uses very low discount rates, which it derives by imposing its own ethical considerations within the framework of social time preference theory.[6] This approach involves the use of

---

4 Ross McKitrick suggests linking a carbon tax to the mean tropical tropospheric anomaly.

5 Wealth should include the stock of natural as well as physical and human resources.

6 This modelling originates in a distinguished line of analysis linking work by

highly stylised long-term economic models that characterise the economy as a smooth set of long-term relationships. It abstracts from uncertainty, leaving issues of risk to be handled separately.[7] Such a deterministic world bears limited resemblance to the market world of risk, uncertainty, successes, mistakes and fluctuations that we inhabit.

Within its narrow limitations, this abstract and mechanical approach allows some key variables to be set out in the form of the 'Ramsey' equation. This points to a discount rate based on (1) pure intergenerational time preference, (2) an assumption as to the future growth of consumption and (3) a figure for the elasticity of marginal utility with respect to consumption. The Stern Review puts the rate of pure intergenerational time preference at 0.1 per cent, different from zero only because of the possibility of the extinction of the human race. It puts the expected growth of consumption at 2 per cent for the current century and 1.3 per cent for the longer future. It puts the utility/consumption elasticity at 1.0. This yields a discount rate of 2.1 per cent for this century and one of 1.4 per cent for the longer-term future.

The rate of pure time preference and the utility/consumption elasticity are both intuitively slippery and largely non-observable. The assumption concerning the growth of consumption should be systematically related to the growth of GDP that drives the growth

---

Irving Fisher and Frank Ramsey with the development of neoclassical balanced-growth steady-state equilibrium models following the work of Robert Solow, Tjalling Koopmans and David Cass. This is not the only way to approach these matters; see, e.g., Scott (1991).

7   Martin Weitzman points out that 'the debate about discounting in climate change centers on the Ramsey equation, which applies only for a deterministic world'.

of greenhouse gas emissions; but such a relationship in the Review is unclear.

The Review argues that pure time preference is an ethical matter, without sufficient recognition that different ethical positions can be justified. The number for the utility/consumption elasticity implies a view about intergenerational distribution, on which views differ, and where the Review's own figure appears inconsistent with the distributional policies that it advocates, namely the desirability of developed countries bearing most of the burden of mitigating climate change.

Further problems arise when the combination of the three numbers in the Ramsey equation diverges from the return on capital in the economy. As the growth models from which they are derived are intended to be simplified representations of market economies, the combination of these parameters should be consistent with the observed returns to capital. While it may be legitimate to speculate about the relative importance of the 'ethical' and 'distributional' components of discount rates, difficulties arise if such arguments lead to the calculation of discount rates that differ markedly from the evidence available from market returns.[8]

If there is such a divergence, a serious problem arises concerning the measurement of opportunity cost. Allowance needs to be made for the difference in the form of a premium – or shadow price – on the cost of displaced investment. This issue is widely recognised and appeared in the global warming literature in a study by William Cline as long ago as 1992 (Cline, 1992). His solution was to apply a shadow price of capital; insofar as mitigation expenditures

---

8   This is argued powerfully by Nordhaus (2007a), and by Weitzman (see below).

displace higher-yielding investments. Their initial costs should be adjusted upwards; he suggests a mark-up of 60 per cent. That would alone shift the Stern Review estimate of the cost of mitigation from 1 per cent of GDP to 1.6 per cent.

The Review fails to address this issue. It relies exclusively on the use of discount rates that overemphasise the cost of any damages resulting from emissions of greenhouse gases while failing to correct for the opportunity cost of action to mitigate them. It also raises serious problems of dual discounting for those concerned with investment appraisal, without any clear guidance on the practical consequences.

The market economy

In a market economy people are compensated for reducing consumption, while the existence of profitable investment opportunities ensures that increases of either physical capital or human capital will increase the income and wealth available for use in the future. Policies for mitigating climate change must fit into the way that markets are already setting patterns of resource use. Any crowding out of investment earning a viable return in the market will reduce the capability of future generations to deal with challenges coming from climate change.

Different people will have different views about using resources now and in the future, depending on their preferences and circumstances.[9] Different types of investment in physical

---

9   These preferences may differ markedly between different people and between the same people at different stages of their lives, as is shown by their willingness to pay very high rates for consumer credit, while receiving much lower rates on savings invested in government bonds.

or human capital will yield different returns, depending on the opportunities for profitable innovation, on macroeconomic conditions and political events. While future generations may face different circumstances and have different capabilities, we can, however, expect them, in most, but perhaps not all, parts of the world, to be considerably better off, on average, than we now are, and to have accumulated much more physical, human and often environmental capital than we now have.[10]

Market rates of discount are determined by the joint effects of the supply of savings, personal and corporate, and by the productivity of capital. In a neoclassical world, in the absence of taxation, when all adjustments have taken place, the marginal rate of interest earned by savers would equal the marginal return on capital.[11]

Pulling together different levels of interest rates, and different returns to capital, in different time periods and in different parts of the world, over a time period during which the resources will be used by generations yet unborn, would be a heroic task. Whatever numbers are used, to get issues into perspective, and to point to sensible direction of policy, their use must always be subjected to sensitivity analyses to test the robustness – or otherwise – of any policy conclusion.

---

10 Economic growth of 2.5 per cent/year involves doubling the standard of living every generation. Over a century, that would involve an increase in living standards by a factor of 12. Provided that people in low-income countries are able to take advantage of the opportunities for economic growth, they can expect a transformation of their living standards – and their capability to deal with problems.

11 In practice continued innovations increase the productivity of capital, often in a clustered way involving turbulence and feedback. Economic growth proceeds not smoothly but, in Schumpeter's phrase, as 'a gale of creative destruction'.

The evidence on returns to capital

For many parts of the world, no reliable estimates are available of the returns that have been experienced on physical, human and, in principle, environmental capital – rates that should influence the discount rates used in studies of climate change. For the USA and the UK, however, such estimates have been made covering a large part of the twentieth century. Provided that markets continue to function well, economic growth should continue and broadly similar returns should continue to accrue.

Evidence of returns to physical capital in the USA and the UK indicates returns over the wide span of the twentieth century of around 5–6 per cent – or possibly more – after adjusting for inflation. Returns to education are comparable with or possibly higher than those to physical capital. Returns to environmental capital are more difficult to ascertain, although there is considerable evidence of environmental improvements, e.g. to air and water quality.[12] The UK experience is similar.[13, 14]

---

12 In his recent study, William Nordhaus notes that 'The real pre-tax return on US non-financial corporations over the last four decades has averaged about 6.6 percent per year, while the returns to US non-financial industries over the 1997–2006 period averaged 8.9 percent per year. Estimated real returns on human capital range from 6 percent per year to 20-plus percent per year depending upon country and time period' (Nordhaus 2007a: 142–3).

13 Returns to equities over much of the twentieth century averaged about 7–8 per cent in real terms. These are figures for viable enterprises and may be biased upwards because they do not take full account of failure. Returns to debt have been much lower, although past figures are confused by changing expectations of inflation. The return now appears to be in the range of 2–3 per cent in real terms for secure bonds.

14 There is a school of thought that believes that for very long-term analyses a lower discount rate should be used. The Stern Review follows this line of thought, arguing both that uncertainty of estimates of the discount rate will increase the farther ahead that one looks and that the rate of world economic growth will fall. But low rates of return are not compatible with dynamic and growing economies.

What will happen in Asia and Africa is more difficult to predict. Japan and Korea are already developed market economies and the Indian and Chinese economies have taken off into a sustained period of per capita growth, fuelled by adequate returns to investment and enterprise. Much of sub-Saharan Africa and parts of the Middle East present a different picture where economic growth is impeded by a range of social and political factors, including malfunctioning governments.

In principle, we should be looking at the 'social', i.e. the overall economic, return, including the taxation of profit, rather than the 'private' return to individual economic actors. Spillover effects can also be important as others may benefit from, for example, investment in educational, health, utility and transport infrastructure.

Any policies to mitigate climate change, but not to adapt to it, must, however, take place at a global level. The returns achieved in successful market economies indicate what a viable position looks like and can, therefore, be used to test policies and to avoid the damage wrought by inadequately thought through policies.

The current debate on climate change is already throwing up options, such as carbon neutrality in one or the other of our daily activities, without raising the question of which would be cost effective, and which could involve a dissipation of resources that could be better used either for the more cost-effective climate change policies, or for ways of increasing our ability to adapt to it. It would be a major mistake to allow the use of specially low rates of discount to push us into projects that would put too many of our eggs into dealing with the future, leaving us impoverished today.[15]

And if growth disappears, so do many of the problems of carbon emissions.

15   As is implied by Partha Dasgupta's comments on the Review, the use of a dis-

The need for sensitivity analysis

Because of the long timescale involved, whatever discount rate is chosen, full sensitivity analysis should be mandatory. This the Stern Review fails to undertake. But we can draw on the work of Martin Weitzman and William Nordhaus and on the limited sensitivities revealed some time after the first publication of the Review.

Martin Weitzman (2007) shows that the discount rate used in the Stern Review, incorporating a near-zero rate of time preference, is the key element leading to the Review's recommendation of urgent and far-reaching action. Going 'right to the target', his own point-guesstimate of what most economists think are the correct (Ramsey) parameter values would be a trio of twos for the pure rate of time preference, the utility/consumption elasticity and for the growth rate of consumption, giving an overall rate of 6 per cent. This is not significantly different from the overall return to capital experienced in the US and UK economies.

Martin Weitzman concludes that:

> The present discounted value of a given global-warming loss
> from a century hence at the non-Stern annual interest rate of
> 6 per cent is one hundredth of the present discounted value
> of the same loss at Stern's centuries-long discount rate of 1.4
> per cent. The disagreement over what interest rate to use
> for discounting is equivalent in its impact to a disagreement
> about the estimated damage costs of global warming a
> hundred years hence of two orders of magnitude.

He argues further that, as the Review estimates the annual costs

count rate significantly lower than those prevailing in the markets for policy analysis is tantamount to asserting that the current level of saving is significantly
too low (Dasgupta, 2007).

of its abatement strategy as being equivalent to about 1 per cent of GDP, the question then becomes whether is it worthwhile to sacrifice 1 per cent of GDP now to remove damages of 5 per cent of GDP a century from now. The benefit-over-cost ratio of such an investment at the Stern Review parameter values would be 4:5 – 'a clear slam-dunk accept'. 'The alternative, non-Stern, values would make it a clear reject' (ibid.: 708).

He argues that the very logic of the type of model used by the Stern Review is that the interest rate for discounting costs and benefits should be the returns to the economy as a whole (ibid.: 712–15): 'If whatever number is used in any reasonable way represents the returns to the economy as a whole then it will completely undo the Review conclusions about drastic consumption smoothing and bring the results back to the much more moderate take-it-more-slowly climate-policy advocated by the mainstream critics of Stern' (ibid.: 712).

William Nordhaus puts a similar case. He concludes that the key difference between his most recent review (2007a) of the position on climate change and that set out in the Review is the choice of a discount rate. For the present century the Stern Review uses a discount rate of 2.1 per cent, while the Nordhaus study uses one of 4 per cent.[16] This difference, which is significantly less than the difference between a social time preference rate of 2 per cent and a market rate of 6 per cent, dramatically changes the present value of the Review's estimate of the damage allegedly caused by climate change because much of the damage would not arise until the end of the present century and would be much more heavily

---

16   Four per cent is a low rate by Nordhaus's criteria, but shows how apparently small differences in discount rates make huge differences to the results of climate change analyses.

discounted by the use of a higher discount rate. At a discount rate of 4 per cent, damage worth £100 in 100 years' time is valued at £2 today; at a rate of 2 per cent it is valued at £14.

The Stern Review is not properly transparent on the discount rates used in its modelling.[17] And the only sensitivities released so far are for a figure of up to 1.5 for both pure time preference and for the consumption elasticity: these imply discount rates sensitivities of 3.5 per cent and 3 per cent respectively, still low numbers. No sensitivity is shown for any combination of them, nor to allow for rates of consumption growth above 1.3 per cent.

Yet this modest use of model simulations substantially reduces the case for action on the scale envisaged by the Review. The first change reduces the estimated damage (present value of loss of GDP) from the 5 per cent quoted as a minimum in the text to 1.4 per cent. The second reduces this 5 per cent figure to 2.9 per cent. As the cost of mitigation is put at 1 per cent of GDP the Review's conclusion could be overturned simply by using higher discount rates without other changes in the numbers used.

Partha Dasgupta commented on the Review shortly after publication that 'the conclusion that I have reached is that the strong immediate action on climate change advocated by the authors is an implication of their views on intergenerational equity; it isn't driven so much by the new climatic facts the authors have stressed'. He continues, 'I can only conjecture that if the consumption elasticity is set in the range 2–4 ... the recommendation would be to do a lot less today on climate change.'[18]

---

17   The parameter values used in the Review were obtained by Christopher Monkton, in a personal communication from HM Treasury.

18   Dasgupta (2007). In a letter to me, he argued that the team should have gone farther than the 1.5 for the utility/consumption elasticity that they used in the subsequent postscript.

In a recent study William Nordhaus (2007b) has illustrated the importance of discount rates using his own model (DICE). This has been done by calculating his study's optimal run – i.e. the computer simulation that shows the optimal rate of moderation of emissions for the damage and cost functions used in the DICE model – using the Stern Review's discount rate. The assumptions are the same as in this first run except that the time preference rate is changed from the 1.5 used in this (Nordhaus's) first run to the 0.1 per cent used in the Stern Review, and his utility/consumption elasticity is changed from the 2 used in this first run to the 1 used in the Review. This dramatically changes the trajectory of climate change policy. The recommended reductions in emissions in the second run are much larger, i.e. reductions of 51 per cent by 2025 – because future damages are in effect treated as occurring today.

The social cost of carbon

Another way of looking at this is through the calculations of 'the social cost of carbon': this measures the present value of additional economic damages now and in the future caused by an additional ton of carbon emissions. This is put in the Nordhaus study at some $30/tonC, compared with the Stern Review's estimate of $80 (ibid.: 165). The postscript to the Stern Review refers to the results of a simulation conducted by Chris Hope, the author of the PAGE2002 model used by the Stern Review team, adopting a discount rate of 4 per cent, published in the *Financial Times* following the initial release of the Review.[19] Chris Hope found that with the higher discount rate the estimate of the social

---

19 www.ft.com/cms/s/444ff4ae-788c-11db-be09-0000779e2340.html. Also Hope (2006).

cost of carbon would fall by just over half to $40 for the Business as Usual (BAU) path explored in the Stern Review. Nordhaus also considers that the major reason for the Review's high social cost of carbon and recommendations for sharp emissions reductions is the use of a low discount rate (Nordhaus, 2007b: 163).

Is there a special 'ethical' element to be taken into account?

The 'ethical' parameters of the Stern Review need their own challenge. There needs to be powerful reasoning behind any departure of social time preference rates from market behaviour and observed returns. And any change in one of the parameters implies changes in one of the others if the resultant rate is to be congruent with the return on capital. If this is not properly followed through, the discount rate will become detached from those used in other parts of the economy.[20]

To use one discount rate for climate change projects and another for other projects requires setting up a complex system of shadow prices to correct for the potential distortion involved in favouring investment in climate change over other investment, or some other forms of detailed microeconomic intervention by government planners.

We also need to ask whether, in a liberal market economy, it would be sensible to hand over the task of determining a rate of time preference to wise men who would be tasked to weigh not only our present preferences and attitudes to future generations

---

20 As already noted, William Cline (Cline, 1992) advocates a low social time preference rate of discount for evaluating climate change expenditures, but faces up to the issue of 'crowding out' by applying a 'shadow price of capital' – suggesting a mark-up of 60 per cent.

but their views and preferences concerning generations future to them.

The 'wise men' do not present us with a clear and agreed position. Wilfred Beckerman and Cameron Hepburn have gone through the arguments that can be used for adopting one 'ethical' position or another and concluded that 'While ... the "revealed ethics" of the marketplace have limited applicability to climate policy, leaving climate ethics up to elites and philosopher-kings is similarly inappropriate ... as, [quoting Isaiah Berlin], disregard for the preferences and interests of individuals alive today in order to pursue some distant social goal that their rulers have claimed is their duty to promote has been a common cause of misery for millions of people throughout the ages.' They argue that 'Stated preference surveys, behavioural experiments, and methods to reveal the social preferences inherent in our social institutions' should be used (Beckerman and Hepburn, 2007).

This would be more consistent with properly engaging the public in analysis rather than rhetoric. It seems likely, however, that increases in living standards through continuation of a dynamic and growing economy with sustainable returns to capital would score well in such questioning. While some tweaking of the figures, up or down, provided by observation and analysis of markets may be justified, it would be a brave, or foolhardy, person who could claim to take on his or her shoulders the framework for deriving, handing down and telling us how to use a world discount rate. It would require either a single world decision-maker or acceptance by people in all countries of a similar set of objectives.[21]

---

21 'The normatively acceptable real interest rates prescribed by philosophers, economists, or the British government are irrelevant to determining the ap-

Much more analysis and informed discussion needs to take place before that would be possible. And any such agreement is more likely to be possible if it is based on numbers that are accepted by analysts and recognised in the markets rather than presumptions that emerge as the latest version of the 'public interest'. As far as economists are concerned, Martin Weitzman argues that '... Stern deserves a measure of *discredit* for giving readers an authoritative-looking impression that seemingly best-available-practice professional economic analysis robustly supports its conclusions instead of more openly disclosing the full extent to which the Review's radical policy recommendations depend on controversial extreme assumptions and unconventional discount rates that most mainstream economists would consider much too low' (Weitzman, 2007: 724).

What flows of resources, i.e. of goods and services, should be discounted at what rate?

The choice of special low discount rates, as recommended in the Stern Review, for expenditures – and other displacements of resources – involves deciding what expenditures and what instruments are designed for climate change rather than other purposes. As virtually all policies in the world of practical politics are designed to serve several objectives, such a test would be subject to endless argument. How, for example, would taxes on motor fuel be classified – are they to reduce emissions, act as a proxy charge for using the highways, to reduce air pollution or what? And within the category of climate change policies, how would

propriate discount rate to use in the actual financial and capital markets of the United States, China, Brazil, and the rest of the world' (Nordhaus, 2007b: 149).

policies to mitigate warming be compared with policies to adapt to warming? Would measures to reduce carbon emissions be assessed at a low discount rate while investment in flood control was assessed at higher ones?[22] And if adaptation investments were to qualify for the low discount rate, how would they be distinguished from other investment? Higher levels of technical skill could improve our capability to adapt, so should they qualify for the low discount rate?[23]

The wider allocation of resources by government that would be made necessary by setting discount rates well below market levels in some areas and correcting the results by specifying shadow prices to allow for the opportunity cost of the resources used could lead to a planning nightmare.[24] Neither the models nor the information to do the job exist, and even if they did the political process would assuredly determine answers that were based on specific (and inconsistent) short-term political desiderata. Such an approach would impoverish us economically, damage individual freedom and, paradoxically, reduce our ability to deal with the consequences of climate change.

---

22 The Review seems ambivalent on this. It argues for a discount rate for 'scenarios' that differs from the 'rate used for a technique of electricity generation' (nuclear power?).

23 The UK Treasury has already entered this area by designating a public sector discount rate of 3.5 per cent – higher than the one used in the Review, but significantly below the productivity of capital. This discount rate is, however, only to be used to influence the capital intensity of investment. Its volume is determined otherwise, by the adoption of public expenditure limits.

24 It is arguable that the use of a widespread carbon tax would deal with this issue, allowing market agents to incorporate the social cost of carbon into their calculations while still using market discount rates. But the Stern Review claims to have identified two 'market failures', one concerning carbon emissions and the other concerning the use of discount rates'. How they would interact and how policies to deal with a combination would operate is left for others to work out.

References

Beckerman, W. and C. Hepburn (2007), *World Economics*, 8(1), January–March.

Cline, William R. (1992), *The Economics of Global Warming*, Washington, DC: Institute of International Economics.

Dasgupta, P. (2007), 'Commentary: the Stern Review's economics of climate change', *National Institute Economic Review*, 199, January.

Hope, C. (2006), 'The marginal impact of CO_2 from PAGE2002: an integrated assessment model incorporating the IPCC's five reasons for concern', *Integrated Assessment*, 6: 19–56.

Munnell, A. and S. Sass (2008), *Working Longer: The Solution to the Retirement Income Challenge*, Washington, DC: Brookings Institution.

Nordhaus, W. D. (2007a), 'A Review of the Stern Review on the Economics of Climate Change', *Journal of Economic Literature*, XLV(3).

Nordhaus, W. D. (2007b), 'The challenge of global warming', *Economic Models and Environmental Policy*, 24 July.

Scott, M. (1991), *A New View of Economic Growth*, Oxford: Clarendon Press.

Weitzman, M. L. (2007), 'Review of the Stern Review on the Economics of Climate Change', *Journal of Economic Literature*, XLV(3).

6 CLIMATE CHANGE, RELIGION AND HUMAN FREEDOM
Alan Peacock[1]

Introduction

Critics of the conventional view that science 'proves' that, given present policies, damaging global warming will occur as a consequence of human actions frequently warn that this view is leading towards adoption of a new secular religion, of a pronounced ascetic character. The 'religious' nature of the campaign is indicated by the raising of barriers to entry, supported by eminent scientists, into critical discussion of the science of climate change. Such criticisms are regarded in much the same way as established religions view heresy. At the same time, supporters of the damaging climate change hypothesis fervently advocate stringent government measures to reduce greenhouse gas emissions which would have a serious impact on individual freedom.

This chapter contends that examination of the analogy with a religious movement, or rather the apocalyptic aspects of some religious beliefs, has much to reveal about the dangers of an uncritical acceptance of this new conventional wisdom.[2] It therefore moves

---

1   The author wishes to thank Ian Byatt, Ian Castles, David Henderson, Nigel Lawson and Colin Robinson for pertinent criticisms of earlier drafts, though not accepting them all.

2   The president of the Czech Republic, Dr Vaclav Klaus, is one of the few political leaders who have rejected the conventional view: see his invited evidence to the US Congressional Committee on Economics and Commerce, March 2007. The

well outside the normal area of discourse of economics, starting from the typologies of organised religion developed by sociologists and originating with Max Weber (an economist in his own right).

A typology of the climate change issue

The typology used here is a crude adaptation of some of the characteristics of apocalyptic aspects of religious belief identified and elaborated by Weber and later writers.[3]

Prophecy

Prophets see the fate of humankind as encapsulated in some measure of changes in its condition as a consequence of its behaviour. In considering this condition, even the earliest prophetic statements about progress towards disaster embodied some material element manifested in plague and famine. The desire to be more specific arose with the growth in scientific knowledge, and movements in the standard of living, as measured by real income per head, have become the point of reference for measurement.[4]

robustness of his opposition is epitomised in his opening statement: 'man-made climate change has become one of the most dangerous arguments aimed at distorting human efforts and public policies ...' For a penetrating examination of the growing politicisation of science in the UK and the EC, with climate change as the major example, see Booker and North (2007), particularly chs 14 and 15.

3   See Gerth and Wright Mills (1947). The sociology of religion is now a well-established branch of sociological investigation. Bruce (2002) offers an admirable account of it. Chapter 7 of the work offers some critical remarks on the application of 'market economics' to the analysis of the demand for religion.

4   Made possible by the refinement of economic statistics, beginning in the nineteenth century with the improvement in the reliability of population censuses and the information derived from the administration of taxes, coupled later with

Because humankind places so much emphasis on the material basis of welfare, it has always been harangued by prophets who have claimed that this materialism endangers survival of the species. There is, however, an interesting difference between older and more recent prophecies. Older prophets visualised, for example, that the worship of the Golden Calf (the symbol of material prosperity) would arouse the wrath of the Deity, who would punish those who strayed from some prescribed moral code. Beginning with Malthus, himself a Church of England parson, it was considered inevitable that the pursuit of material wealth would bring about its own demise unless a particular moral code were followed. The growth of material wealth would rise with population through the growth in the labour supply and the increase in the capital stock. The stimulation that material wealth would give to population increase would eventually result in a rise in the labour supply outstripping the rise in cooperant factors of production, causing a fall in the rate of economic growth and, in extreme situations, a fall in real incomes to subsistence levels.[5]

---

much more careful definition of the meaning of 'real income' and social accounting terms in general. Different definitions of 'real income' bedevil discussion of the climate change problem and international standards of living. See Castles and Henderson (2003: 415–35). The recognition by the House of Lords Select Committee on Economic Affairs of the importance of this issue is found in ch. 4 of their *Report on the Economics of Climate Change* (vol. 1: House of Lords Paper 12–1, Session 2005–06). See also below.

5   The Malthusian bogey still haunts analysis of human 'progress', largely nowadays among natural scientists with a prophetic bent. The intellectual influence is derived from Darwin, who was a great believer in Malthusianism as an explanation of population growth in the animal kingdom. The contemporary debate between natural scientists, similarly influenced, and social scientists is fully discussed in Lomborg (2001). As long as 50 years ago, the author recalls taking part in a similar debate with Sir Charles Darwin, grandson of his more famous namesake, at a conference organised by the Institute of Biology. See Peacock (1955).

In the Malthusian system, human actions are judged by appeal to some extraterrestrial authority and not by humans themselves, provided that the authority of those who interpret the judgements (Moses, for example) is accepted. The source of the judgement on human actions has now changed, however: population disaster is now regarded as a consequence of human weakness and ignorance and not, as in Malthus's own interpretation, such weakness and ignorance fuelled by 'immoral' behaviour in producing large families and thus the lack of 'moral restraint', as prescribed by Christian doctrine. The specification of remedies and their implementation now lies firmly in the hands of man himself.

Sin, salvation and heresy

Sin is recognised in a transgression of some fundamental law which is designed to separate the 'sheep', who conform to the law, and the 'goats', who question or even reject its provenance. A prophet, followed by a group of disciples, is usually recognised as the source of transmission of the content of the moral order, his or her authority often being buttressed by the claim to have miraculous powers, as evidenced in Moses's parting of the waters. The subsequent history of the translation of the moral order into regulation of the lives of those professing belief in its principles shows remarkable similarity between different religions of a hegemonic character, based on revelation – the need to establish a ritual of worship covering all stages of the life of individuals; the formulation of practices governing all aspects of individual life from the food eaten to sexual behaviour; the prescription of laws to enforce the moral order and to resolve disputes between its adherents; and the devising of sanctions against those who lapse from or reject the theocratic rule. The civil authority, from the monarchy downwards, must bend to the moral order and act as an agent of enforcement through military action and criminal law. Perhaps, above all, religious conformity must be a cardinal element in school and higher education.

We can find parallels between this typology and that of the present worldwide interest in environmental questions in general and climate change in particular, where the canons of behaviour originate from man himself (even if sometimes endorsed by, for example, Christian preachers). The commandment that we should change our ways and protect Planet Earth from the 'ravages' of the actions of sovereign consumers and private producers trying to satisfy their wishes is strongly entrenched in the mindsets of those who claim to be our legitimate political representatives in national and international affairs.

Moreover, this mindset has been translated into the transfer of power to the United Nations (UN) for the responsibility of formulating policy prescriptions, thus enlarging its role beyond the resolution of international disputes that could (and do) lead to military and trade wars, to cover more direct ways of intervening in the personal lives of its members' citizens. Of course, international organisations promulgating principles of action that are meant to have a pronounced influence on individual behaviour are formally the creatures of the members of the UN and its satellites such as UNESCO and FAO. As public choice analysis makes clear, however, their powerful bureaucracies not only play a crucial role in the formulation of principles but also conduct the investigations that are designed to guide their application. As such they are far removed from the pressures of re-election that apply to national politicians; and politicians, if not their officials, are more accessible to and influenced by interest groups.[6]

A prime example of an international organisation that has gained considerable influence on policy is the UN's Intergovernmental Panel on Climate Change (IPCC), which acts as if it had acquired a monopoly of expertise in the preparation of forecasts of climate change and its effects. As indicated in David Henderson's chapter in this volume, its models continue to support the contentions that greenhouse gas emissions are the major cause of climate change, that emissions are closely associated with the growth and changing structure of rich industrial countries, and that climate change will be detrimental to the world's prosperity and will have a more marked effect on that of poorer countries – unless, of course, collective action is introduced to cut the growth in emissions.[7]

The IPCC's public statements bear comparison with those of the prophets of old. It unilaterally defines the relationship between human action and its 'sinful' results in the form of the cataclysmic effect of anthropogenic global warming. Of course, its utterances are claimed to have the backing of a substantial consensus of

---

6   For an excellent short survey of the empirical support for this statement, see Vaubel (2004; and references therein). *The Economist* (4 August 2007) contained an advertisement for the post of Assistant Secretary-General of the United Nations Environment Programme (UNEP). It is prefaced with the statement: 'UNEP is the leading global environmental authority within the United Nations promoting the environmental dimension of sustainable development and *serving as the authoritative advocate for the global environment*' (emphasis added).

7   For useful detail on the role and development of the IPCC and critique of its conclusions, see Bradley (2003: pt IV and *passim*). For further detail, see the excellent critique of the 'gap' between the 'consensus' evidence and its interpretation in the Stern Review and the IPCC itself in Henderson (forthcoming). Essential reading for those interested in the politics as well as the science penetrating the IPCC procedures is Holland (2007).

natural scientists, and are not derived from some form of mysticism designed to be the source of divine revelation. It is already beginning to point the way to 'salvation' by prescribing the methods for ensuring compliance with the wishes of those countries seeking an international agreement on tackling climate change. Those who express doubts and reservations about the IPCC's conclusions risk being charged with the equivalent of 'heresy'.

Crime and punishment

In established religions, there is usually some allowance made for those who confess that they have broken the moral laws and are willing to submit to some form of punishment in expiation, geared to the magnitude of the sin. Human weakness may be treated with various degrees of leniency, but human obstinacy that questions the assumptions made by a religion on man's nature and practices and the ethical basis of its faith must be firmly opposed and, in circumstances where freedom of choice of religion is prohibited, must be rooted out. Severity in this process of elimination of opposition has extended from engagement in public debate with opponents to the use of torture and execution, *'pour encourager les autres'*.

Coming back to Dr Klaus's fears, an interesting issue is whether we now see the beginnings of a secular version of a moral code in which the necessity for controlling climate change, and even particular methods of control, is regarded as imperative. If such a code is appearing, and as a consequence there is a list (albeit implied) of 'heresies', significant additional constraints on individual behaviour may appear and Dr Klaus's fears should be matters of serious concern. In the past, religious beliefs have been used to suppress human freedom – though arguably mainstream religious beliefs are perfectly compatible with human freedom. There is a case for saying that, at the present time, climate change is being used, as religious beliefs have been used in centuries past, as a rationale for curtailing freedom.

Climate change and individual freedom

As well as considering Dr Klaus's worries from the standpoint of the sociology of religion, it is useful also to place present-day views about the effects of climate change in historical context by considering some noteworthy features of the growth of the supply of science and its effect on views about climate change.

1) *The growth in scientific knowledge that gradually replaced unprovable prophecy that took it for granted that the earth was the centre of the universe.*
This is a remarkable story, given the intense opposition of religious orders in the power structure of governments.[8] In striking contrast to the situation today, famous scientists, such as Halley and Newton, relied on the Crown and their advisers to protect them from attempts to have them branded as heretics.

---

8   The author is acutely conscious of the personal sacrifices this entailed, being a Corresponding Fellow of the Italian Academy (Accademia Nazionale dei Lincei) founded by Galileo and his scientific colleagues. After Galileo was forced to recant his views on the orbiting of the earth round the sun, the Accademia was banned by the Pope. Restored after the Risorgimento in the nineteenth century, it was again dissolved by Mussolini because of its refusal to expel members who opposed fascism and then revived after World War II owing to the sterling efforts of Croce and Einaudi, who became the president of the Italian republic. For a further reminder of the risks of persecution by the Church faced by British natural scientists, see Kealey (2005: 44–7).

2) *The reduction in the costs of communication of scientific ideas.*
This was produced by the expansion of the popular press from the late nineteenth century onwards and the growth in knowledge of the public through public education and the popularity of local scientific societies.[9] Today there is an extensive international market in popular scientific periodicals, novels and topical broadcast programmes.

For many years, scientific pronouncements have been regarded as newsworthy. For example, on 21 June 1898 the *Washington Post* contained the following report under the heading 'Only 400 years': 'Lord Kelvin, the eminent scientist, has not added to the mirthfulness of nations by announcing that in four hundred years the oxygen now virtually free in our atmosphere will be used up, and the inhabitants of the earth will die of suffocation from carbonic acid gas ...'[10]

The sheaf of reports on the inferences drawn from detailed experimental and empirical investigation, particularly if they attribute some natural disaster to global warming, now receive, however, more respectful attention from the popular media than they did in Kelvin's day. In short, supply has created its own demand, as in many other products or services that have become widely available.

---

9 In the eighteenth and early nineteenth centuries, literary journalists often made fun of the claims of science. Of particular interest is Samuel Johnson's young Ethiopian prince, Rasselas, in the novel of that name, who escapes his family in order to see the world and becomes friendly with an ageing astronomer of awesome reputation. The astronomer takes him into his confidence and explains that his main worry is that when he dies there will be no one to look after the universe! The same illusion can be found among those who spend their professional lives as economic forecasters and may come to believe that somehow they control the economic variables whose movements they attempt to predict.

10 I am indebted to Professor Oliver Penrose, FRS, for this information.

3) *The tendency of scientists to advocate government 'remedies'.*
Public interest in the contribution of science lies primarily in what
it can tell us about the material basis of human welfare. Science
offers not only new discoveries but the prospect of avoiding
problems that appear to be detrimental to human welfare, such as
'overpopulation' and 'over-exploitation' of non-renewable sources
of energy. As these activities seem directly controllable by human
beings, it is inviting to scientists, anxious to show how their efforts
can help humankind and tempted to predict what would happen
if human beings do not control their numbers or economise in
non-renewables, to advocate remedies that involve government
action. The fact that their predictions have gone horribly wrong
and persistently so (see Russell Lewis's chapter in this volume)
has not prevented a coalescence of scientific endeavour to offer
a further sensational explanation of how humankind endangers
itself through the generation of greenhouse gases and their baleful
influence on the atmosphere. In making their prescriptions,
scientists tend to ignore important issues such as the relative effi-
ciencies of governmental and non-governmental measures and
unresolved questions centring on whether or not industry itself
and those affected by pollution can solve the question of cost and,
if need be, that of compensatory arrangements without recourse
to elaborate government intervention.[11]

The present demand for action on climate change is closely
bound up with the development of science, including its contribution to rapid changes in broadcasting technology, and with the
respect now accorded to the pronouncements of scientists. The
striking increase in prosperity in Western-type democracies, the

---

11   For further discussion, see Peacock (2003) and references therein.

concomitant growth in demand of the public for scientific knowledge in popular form, and the combination of a wider spread of education with a wider franchise have been other powerful influences.

Although one can trace public concern for the physical environment back at least to Victorian times,[12] its operational significance in public political support for control of the environment is a fairly recent phenomenon. Public choice analysis would indicate that if there are votes for elected representatives in control of the physical environment, such votes may be consolidated by drawing on the consciousness of the public that there is strong support among eminent scientists for stringent measures to control climate change. The growing acceptance of such measures is all the more remarkable given that such measures impose costs on voters now in the expectation of benefits very far into the future. A somewhat cynical view might be that fear offers a useful strategy for diverting attention away from other worries about everyday life ascribed to government inefficiency or neglect.

Is individual freedom under threat?

In considering Dr Klaus's striking claim that environmentalism is replacing Marxism as the ideological opponent of liberalism, one has to emphasise that the debate is not about economic systems that are based on global economic planning versus the capitalist system.

It is sometimes claimed that 'uncontrolled pursuit of profit'

---

12 Economists may remember the purple passages in Mill (1848: Bk IV, ch. VI) on the limits to economic growth, and his plea for preserving the natural environment. See further Peacock (2003: 2–3).

has led to methods of wealth creation that ignore the 'negative externalities' created in the form of various forms of pollution, with carbon emissions and other greenhouse gases now ascribed to 'capitalist' greed. Capitalism cannot, however, be so clearly identified with adverse climate change. The volume of pollution may be a positive function of economic growth but economic growth, as conventionally measured by a national income indicator, is independent of the dominant economic system in a particular country, whether capitalist, socialist or 'mixed'. If there are any marked differences between the 'pollution coefficients' under different forms of economic organisation, the reason will lie primarily in the composition of the capital stock. We would expect that major economies which in the twentieth century were 'planned' (such as China and Russia) would have older capital stocks, implying (other things being equal) higher pollution per unit of output than those in contemporary Western-type economies.

In liberal political philosophy, the starting point is that individual freedom is the goal of policy, recognising that the term is difficult to define with any precision and that one can never be certain that the chosen means of achieving individual freedom will work as devised and that, as individual freedom entails equality of political rights, the aim and the methods will be acceptable to those exercising these rights. If such methods are rejected by the electorate, the only remedy for the liberal is to try persuading voters that they are wrong.

There is a marked contrast between a liberal approach to the issue of climate change and the prevailing doctrine that dominates the policies now being adumbrated for worldwide application which assume that the scientific evidence is watertight. The issue under discussion, however, as raised by Dr Klaus, is whether the attempts to pin down the large majority of nations to accepting these policies represent a kind of ideological struggle. The analysis in this chapter confirms that there are indeed features of the climate change debate that support his case.

There are two such features in particular. The first is that, taken in the round, the adoption by governments of the IPCC's position and the alleged 'consensus' view on the immediacy of global warming and its supposed detrimental effects on human welfare amount to registration as members of a movement with all the main characteristics of a religion. Furthermore, this movement does not permit competition from alternative 'religions' – that is, from codes of moral practice that offer a different path to 'salvation'. In economists' language, an attempt is being made by influential natural scientists, notably in the UK, to claim that 'freedom of entry' into the arena of serious scientific discussion of climate change is to be strongly resisted. Of course, the situation has not yet been reached where one is absolutely forbidden from expressing a dissenting view. Nevertheless, support for climate change policies that entail a panoply of controls of individual behaviour in the name of 'saving the planet' embraces some of the top brass of the Royal Society, who appear to be using the professional authority of the Society to conduct what amounts to a witch-hunt of scientists of equal distinction who dissent from their conclusions. This was particularly notable in the Royal Society's attempt to stop Exxon/Mobil from funding those organisations which, in the view of the Royal Society, promoted a position that exaggerated the extent of uncertainty about the impact of greenhouse gas emissions.[13]

---

13   See, for example, the original correspondence at http://royalsociety.org/land-ing.asp?id=1278.

At least as serious an attempt to suppress 'heresies' occurred when Bjorn Lomborg's book *The Sceptical Environmentalist* (2001) was published. Interestingly, Lomborg does not dissent radically from the consensus views on climate science, suggesting that even minor transgressions from doctrine are regarded as heresy. Lomborg does dissent, however, from the view that the existence of man-made warming necessarily justifies wide-ranging government action because he believes that such action might prejudice the living standards and environment of people who are poor today. A large number of scientists from a number of different countries tried to get Cambridge University Press (CUP) to withdraw Lomborg's book from publication (effectively to pulp it), despite the fact that it had gone through the most rigorous process of peer review. The pre-publication reviewers of Lomborg's book had a variety of perspectives on the global warming debate, and were highly qualified, and they all regarded the book as an important contribution to the debate. The specific means by which they put pressure on CUP were most certainly reminiscent of aspects of the Inquisition.[14] A third example, less well documented, of the attempt to suppress 'heresies' relates to the recent publication of Nigel Lawson's book (2008), which, according to the author, was rejected by every British publisher before being accepted by a US publisher.

There are two disturbing aspects to these kinds of activities. The first is the refusal to engage in serious discussion of counter-arguments to the science, including the economics, of climate change.[15] The second is their conspiratorial view of the motivation

14   These incidents have been fully and meticulously documented in Harrison (2004: 357–68).

15   Readers can judge for themselves by the articles on both the science and econom-

of their intellectual critics and opponents.[16] A further strategy entails the attempt to extend the ban on freedom of entry into both the analysis and policy of climate change discussion by the formation of a professional cartel of National Academies of Science and the constant repetition of the mantra that 'consensus' among scientists, whatever that implies, is firm evidence that their predictions of impending, though distant, disaster must therefore be sound.

Another disturbing development is the deliberate attempt to impregnate school education not only with a sensationalist approach to the science of global warming but also with a secularist moral philosophy. Both produce the modern equivalent of a religious movement that cannot countenance any competition – there is only one route to 'salvation'. There is growing evidence in the UK that this form of environmentalism is replacing other forms of teaching on ethical issues, whatever their particular religious or humanistic origins. There can be no objection to explaining how our individual actions affect the welfare of others and offering homely examples that may encourage healthy attitudes towards,

ics of climate change, following the appearance of the Stern Review, in *World Economics* (7(2), 2006, and 8(1), 2007).

16 Expressed by senior figures in the Royal Society in different ways, depending on their audience. Sir David King is reasonably polite about opposition to the establishment view in his evidence to the House of Lords Select Committee on Economic Affairs, vol. 2, Evidence, pp. 96–106. Sir Martin Rees, president of the Royal Society, in his speculations offered to a more general public on the survival prospects of the human race, actually describes Dr Bjorn Lomborg, author of *The Sceptical Environmentalist* (2001), as 'an anti-gloom environmental propagandist' (Rees, 2003: 109). The prize for taking a conspiratorial view of dissentients must be awarded to Lord May (2007), previous president of the Society. Ian Castles has reminded me that back in 2001 Lord May successfully canvassed several national academies to have them denounce those governments that did not accept the establishment view that entailed support for the Kyoto Protocol.

say, waste disposal and energy conservation. It is another matter altogether to claim that those who have doubts about the timing and extent of climate change are 'mad, bad and dangerous to know'.[17] Those of a liberal disposition may well conclude that there is evidence that the progress of environmentalism as an ideological force has reached the stage where its practical influence has become close to that of a monotheist religion. It would certainly be a strange irony to find that the Royal Society had now become enjoined to root out the 'heresies' of sceptics, having been itself accused of heresy in the years of its origin.[18]

Optimists will claim that 'true science', including economics, will win through in the end and before too much damage is done. National and international governmental measures, based on long-term forecasts of climate change and incomplete models of the causal relationships between greenhouse gas emissions, climate change and economic consequences, will nevertheless be

17 Mr David Miliband, when Secretary of State for the Environment, Food and Rural Affairs, claimed that 'the science has been decided and the economics will follow'. It was Mr Miliband who persuaded the Labour government to distribute a CD to all British state schools of Al Gore's tendentious film *An Inconvenient Truth*, now glamorised by the award to him of the Nobel Peace Prize. Even Lord May has called Gore's work 'glossed-up Power Point presentation' (2007: 3). Presumably Lord May would agree with Mr Justice Burton's High Court decision that this film should not be shown in schools without a hearing given to the other side of the argument.

18 In June 2007, the Royal Society issued *Climate Change Controversies: A Simple Guide*, particularly commended by its president, Lord Rees (see his letter to *The Times*, 24 October 2007). It is designed as a corrective to 'those who seek to distort and undermine the science of climate change' (Preface). No empirical estimates are given to support the predictions of global warming; the members of the Royal Society responsible for its drafting are not identified; nor are those whom they attack. The reader would be tempted to conclude that the *Guide* reads like a latter-day papal encyclical, but with the difference that encyclicals do not claim infallibility. I am glad to find a simultaneous criticism by Freeman Dyson (Dyson, 2008), one of the USA's top physicists and, significantly, also an FRS.

effective in changing behaviour without significant adverse effects on freedom. No doubt that is a possible outcome and I hope these optimistic expectations will be fulfilled. But, on a more sober view, we should be wary of the dangers to individual freedom inherent in the present consensus about prospective climate change and how to deal with it.

References

Booker, C. and R. North (2007), *Scared to Death: From BSE to Global Warming*, London: Continuum.

Bradley, R. L., Jr (2003), *Climate Alarmism Reconsidered*, London: Institute of Economic Affairs.

Bruce, S. (2002), *God Is Dead: Secularization in the West*, Oxford: Blackwell.

Castles, I. and D. Henderson (2003), 'Economics, emission scenarios and the work of the IPCC', *Energy and Environment*, 14(4): 415–35.

Dyson, F. (2008), 'The question of global warming', *New York Review of Books*, 12 June, pp. 43–5.

Gerth, H. and C. Wright Mills (eds) (1947), *From Max Weber: Essays on Sociology*, Pt III, London: Kegan Paul.

Harrison, C. (2004), 'Peer review, politics and pluralism', *Environmental Science and Policy*, 7.

Henderson, D. (forthcoming), 'Government and climate change issues: the case for rethinking', *World Economics*.

Holland, D. (2007), 'Bias and concealment in the IPCC process: the "hockey-stick" affair and its implications', *Energy and Environment*, 18(7/8).

Kealey, T. (2005), 'Bacon's shadow', *Prospect*, October.

Lawson, N. (2008), *An Appeal to Reason: A cool-headed look at global warming*, London: Duckworth.

Lomborg, B. (2001), *The Sceptical Environmentalist: Measuring the Real State of the World*, Cambridge: Cambridge University Press.

May, Lord (2007), 'Respect the facts', *Times Literary Supplement*, 6 April, pp. 3–4.

Mill, J. S. (1848), *Political Economy*.

Peacock, A. (1955), 'Economic theory and the concept of an optimum population' in Cragg and Pirie (eds), *The Numbers of Animals and Man*, Edinburgh: Oliver and Boyd.

Peacock, Sir A. (2003), *The Political Economy of Sustainable Development*, David Hume Institute.

Rees, Sir M. (2003), *Our Final Century*, London: Heinemann.

Vaubel, R. (2004), 'International organization', in C. K. Rowley and F. Schneider (eds), *The Encyclopedia of Public Choice*, vol. 2, Dordrecht, London and Boston, MA: Kluwer.

7 WHICH POLICY TO ADDRESS CLIMATE CHANGE?
Julian Morris

Falsehoods and non sequiturs abound in discussions of climate change: often they are found together. So, for example, it is frequently asserted that 'the science is settled' (a falsehood) and that, *therefore*, 'drastic measures are required to avert catastrophe' (a non sequitur). In this chapter, I briefly consider the question of what we know about climate change, before moving on to discuss a range of policy options that might be considered in response to what we know.

What do we know about the science of climate change?

The science of climate change is far from settled. Arguably, it will never be settled. If climate is indeed a chaotic system,[1] as it seems to be, then it is unlikely that we will ever be able perfectly to describe all the relationships between different variables in the system. Nor are we likely ever to have sufficiently accurate measurements of those variables at any point in time such that we would be able accurately to forecast far into the future. The best that we can hope for is models that will provide estimates of boundary values for the system. But we are a long way from a model that does this accurately (Green and Armstrong, forthcoming).

---

1 That is, chaotic in the technical sense of the word.

One of the reasons we are so far from having reliable estimates, even of boundary values, for the climate is that climate science is a relatively young discipline. But it is developing rapidly: hundreds of papers are published every year addressing all aspects of climate, from analysis of Antarctic ice cores, to models of the behaviour of water molecules in the tropopause. In contrast to the claims of consensus, however, there continues to be substantial disagreement on many important aspects of the science of climate change.

In the past few years, there have been major disagreements over many issues, including:

- The variability of global mean temperature since AD 1000, with some analysts claiming that the recent rise in temperature is unprecedented during that period (Mann et al., 1998, 1999), while others have shown that no such conclusion can be drawn: the result is an artefact of poorly constructed statistical modelling techniques (McIntyre and McKitrick, 2003; Wegman et al., 2006).
- The variation in (North Atlantic) hurricane numbers and intensity since about 1900, with some analysts claiming that hurricanes have become more common and more intense (Emanuel, 2005a, 2005b), while others have pointed out that such a result ignores earlier data that show that hurricane numbers follow a cycle and do not increase in number as a result of global mean temperature (Goldenberg et al., 2001; Pielke, 2005; Landsea, 2005; Vecchi and Soden, 2007).
- The extent to which human-induced warming has and will affect the incidence of vector-borne disease, with some analysts claiming that warming has already caused a rise in

malaria (Patz et al., 2002; Epstein, 1998; Haines and Patz, 2004), while others have shown that this is contradicted by the evidence (Dye and Reiter, 2000; Reiter, 2001, 2005).

The parameters of current climate 'forecasting' models are derived from moderately accurate data going back just over a century. Graphical representations typically show the relationship between historical temperature data and model outputs. Given that the models are parameterised using the same data with which they are compared, it is not surprising that they achieve a reasonable fit. This is no indication of their ability to forecast the future. To the extent that any model forecasts have been tested (i.e. comparing forecasts to data outside the sample used to parameterise the model), they have performed poorly, with actual temperatures coming in at the very bottom of the range of forecasts, suggesting upward bias in the models (Lindzen, 2005; Houghton, 2005; Watson et al., 2001).

To complicate matters, such forecasts of future temperatures are necessarily dependent upon accurate forecasts of future emissions of greenhouse gases (GHGs), which are inevitably no more reliable than any other forecast of human behaviour. Anyone familiar with economic forecasts knows just how poor their record is in forecasting even a year ahead, let alone a decade ahead. No serious economist would try to forecast a century ahead because they know that practically all the variables affecting the structure of the economy are likely to change over that period. For example, it is difficult to imagine what a forecaster might have come up with in 1908 had they attempted to predict the state of the world in 2008, but it is unlikely to have been anything like the world we actually inhabit. Alarmists of the day might have been concerned about the availability of coal and the implications of rising levels of horse dung.

Furthermore, it is plausible that in the next 50 years various technologies will be developed that will result in dramatic reductions in greenhouse gas emissions as well as cost savings. If so, the relationship between economic growth and emissions will be quite different from that envisaged in the more alarmist IPCC scenarios. It may be that some additional incentives are necessary to stimulate those developments – about which more later – but it is also plausible that such changes will occur spontaneously.

Consider some of the new technologies developed during the past half-century which, often in combinations not envisaged at the time of their development, have had unimaginable impacts on our lives. A good example is the laser, which turned out to have uses far beyond those originally envisaged when it was developed in the late 1950s. Lasers are now widely used to write and retrieve data on optical disks. In addition, and perhaps more importantly, they are used to transmit data through a worldwide network of fibre-optic cables. In combination with widespread ownership of personal computers, a set of protocols that enable efficient and effective transmission of data (TCP/IP), and programs that enable user-friendly data transmission, lasers have transformed the way information is transmitted.

In the process, these technologies have substantially reduced the resources required to record and transmit information. Emails save not only on paper but on oil and other resources that are used to cart letters and packages from one place to another. Downloading songs reduces the amount of resources required to deliver music from the producer to the consumer (including the resources embodied in an LP or CD, as well as the resources required to move physical discs from manufacturer to wholesaler to retailer to consumer). Yet data recording, retrieval and transmission were not envisaged as one of the uses for lasers when they were first developed.

Given the likelihood of similar – and similarly unimaginable – combinations of innovations occurring over the course of the next 50 years, it seems the height of arrogance to suggest that we might realistically predict future emissions in any meaningful way. It can fairly be asserted, therefore, that estimates of future global warming are subject to considerable uncertainty.

'Insuring' against global warming

The substantial uncertainty relating to the extent and impact of current and future anthropogenic global warming (AGW) has been interpreted by some as justification for taking urgent action (Stern et al., 2006). The argument is made that since we do not know how bad future warming will be, it is worthwhile investing an amount now to prevent harms in the future. Sometimes this is described as an 'insurance policy'. For most proposed policy responses, this description is inaccurate and misleading.

If we knew that the policy would pay out in the future in response to specific but unforeseen events materialising, the term 'insurance' would be correct. If we knew that the policy would substantially reduce the probability of specified harms occurring, or substantially reduce the extent of those harms should they occur, the term would also be correct. Most climate-related policies advocated under the header of 'insurance' do neither, however.

For the most part, advocates of 'insurance' against climate

change argue simply that the threat of dangerous climate change justifies limiting human emissions of GHGs such as methane and carbon dioxide. Rarely is any effort made to examine the relative merits of alternative policies. When it is, the conclusion is usually swiftly arrived at that the possibility of alternatives, such as adaptation or geoengineering, must not be used as an excuse not to reduce GHG – or even more specifically CO_2 – emissions.

Given the uncertainty of the relationship between GHG concentrations and climate, it is far from clear that even drastic reductions in GHG emissions will have much impact on the climate. Meanwhile, Lomborg (2001: 304) estimates that the Kyoto Protocol, if adhered to strictly by all signatories until 2100, would delay the warming predicted by the IPCC by six years (about 6 per cent). Notwithstanding the doubtful validity of the IPCC's predictions, that does not sound like a very effective insurance policy.

Consider the following analogy. Suppose that we plan to take a trip on a highway with our young daughter. We want to protect our daughter from experiencing a serious head injury during the journey and are offered two ways in which we might achieve that. First, we could put her in a high-backed booster seat and ensure that the seat belt is correctly fitted. Second, we could reduce our speed by 6 per cent, from 50 to 47 kilometres per hour. Evidence suggests that the booster seat and belt will substantially reduce the likelihood of severe injuries during a crash (Durbin et al., 2003; Arbogast et al., 2005). By comparison, the reduction in speed by 3 kilometres per hour will make little difference to the probability of crashing and practically no difference to the probability of head injury should a crash take place (e.g. Moore et al., 1995; Morrison, 2001). Of course, we could put our daughter in a booster safety seat *and* reduce our speed, but the net effect will be little different from simply putting her in the seat.

To those who say to the Lomborgian criticism, 'Yes, but that's because we're not doing enough to slow emissions of greenhouse gases,' here's the rub: the slower you make the car go, the longer it takes to arrive at the end of the journey; and if the journey is worthwhile (which presumably it is), then that may well be a bad thing.

Suppose we are driving our sick daughter to hospital for an urgent operation. The effect of slowing our speed is to increase the likelihood that we arrive too late for the operation and our daughter dies. Now, while reducing our speed by 5 kilometres per hour may reduce that possibility less than if we slow the car to a crawl, it nevertheless undeniably increases the overall probability of her dying (the reduction in probability of arriving at the hospital on time far outweighs the minuscule reduction in the probability of crashing). Clearly, reducing the speed of the car to, say, 30 kph will have a substantial impact on the probability that we will arrive in time to save our daughter.

Applying this reasoning to the climate change problem: if we try to reduce emissions of greenhouse gases too dramatically, we will slow the economy down and that will harm people both directly and indirectly. Meanwhile, if we slow emissions by 6 per cent or so, we will have little impact on the likelihood of catastrophe but will still hamper economic growth.

It is said that the people most likely to be affected by climate change are the poor. This is plausible, since the poor are currently most subject to the whims of the climate (drought, flood, heat, cold, storms, and so on) and are less inherently resilient to change. So, if as a result of restricting emissions of GHGs we slow the economy generally, which is likely regardless of the extent of the emissions reduction but is certain for large reductions, we will almost certainly slow down the progress of the poor. In essence, we will condemn them to continued suffering.

Adaptation: insuring against the impacts of climate change

When considering the best policy to address climate change, it seems reasonable to begin by asking what impact climate change is likely to have. The Civil Society Coalition on Climate Change recently commissioned three papers that seek to answer that question. The first (Southgate and Songhen, 2007) looks at the impact on agriculture (and food) and forestry. The second (Reiter, 2007) looks at the impact on human health. The third (Goklany, 2007) looks at the impact of natural disasters.

Doug Southgate and Brent Songhen (2007) looked at how food production and forestry have changed in the past 100 years and how they might change in the coming century in response to a 1–4° Celsius rise in global mean temperature. After showing that the past 100 years have seen a dramatic rise in productivity in both agriculture and forestry, they conclude that the impact of even a 4° Celsius rise in temperature is unlikely to reduce productivity considerably. The reason is simple: as long as individuals and companies continue to be able to make investments in the development of new technologies, agricultural and forestry productivity will continue to outpace population growth. There may be some changes in the value of land in different parts of the world, but the net effect of climate change is likely to be small compared with the net effect of technological change.

One caveat is worth making, however. There are barriers to adaptation, many (perhaps most) of which come from government intervention of one kind or another. For example, government ownership of land and water leads to perverse, inefficient and often environmentally less suitable uses of them. When land and water are owned privately, the owners have incentives to put those resources to their highest-valued use: that often means putting in place effective conservation measures, using water efficiently, putting in place firebreaks in forests, and so on. Government regulations on land uses often have a similarly detrimental impact, since they preclude many private sector innovations. Likewise, government subsidies often have perverse consequences, such as encouraging the production of crops unsuitable to the terrain and over-abstraction of water. Southgate and Songhen argue that adaptation will take place most rapidly and at least cost if government gets out of the way.

Paul Reiter (2007) analysed the supposed impacts of climate change on health. He found that, contrary to claims made by Epstein (1998), Patz et al. (2002) and the WHO (2005), rates of malaria have not risen as a result of climate change. Rather, in wealthy countries, malaria rates have declined dramatically as a result of a combination of, *inter alia*, changes in animal husbandry practices (people no longer live close to animals), drainage of swamps (where mosquitoes breed), the use of insecticides and larvicides, and the use of air conditioning. Meanwhile, in poorer countries, malaria rates declined after about 1960, in large part as a result of using DDT and other insecticides, but are now rising again, in large part because of reduced usage of DDT.

Other health impacts are also highly dependent on wealth, with people in richer countries generally being far less susceptible to death as a result of extreme temperatures than people in poor countries (Keatinge, 2004; Rayner and Malone, 1998). Thus, an increase in wealth is, by itself, likely to reduce the rate of mortality from extreme temperatures because people will be better able to afford clean and efficient heating and cooling systems, as well as having greater access to medical facilities. But increased wealth also brings the capacity to invest in other strategic disease-reducing activities, such as more effective preventive measures for vector-borne diseases.

Notwithstanding the importance of enabling wealth genera-tion, there are other measures that, if taken now and over the course of the next few decades, will dramatically reduce the likelihood that any AGW would cause an increase in mortality. Those measures include expanding programmes that have been demonstrated to reduce the incidence of diseases such as malaria. For example, spraying the inside walls of huts with small quanti-ties of DDT has been shown to reduce malaria without adversely affecting human health or the environment (Attaran et al., 2000; Roberts et al., 2000; WHO, 2006).

Indur Goklany (2007) shows that mortality and mortality rates from weather-related natural disasters have declined dramatically over the past century. The reasons for this are many and varied but include increased wealth, better building materials, and more reliable warning systems. While the economic damage done by such events has risen, the main reason for this is that wealth has increased both in aggregate and on average. Goklany shows that as a proportion of total wealth in the USA, the impact of extreme weather events has remained largely constant over the past century.

In sum, if we are concerned about the impact of gradual

climate change, then we should focus on policies that can reduce the harms people face today that might be made worse in the future. Creating an environment in which economic development can take place seems in general the best form of insurance, since it will enable people who are currently at the whim of the weather to diversify their economic activities and thereby become more robust in the face of all manner of future challenges.

As Southgate and Songhen point out, reducing government control over land and water resources would enable people better to identify ways of managing those resources in sustainable ways. Removing subsidies and other interventions that provide incentives for the use of flood plains for building also seems sensible. Meanwhile, specific policies aimed at reducing exposure to various pathogens and other causes of ill health may be desirable – but for the most part these would take the form of removing perverse interventions and providing an enabling environment for positive interventions to occur.

How should society address the threat of catastrophe?

Adaptation may well be the most cost-effective option for addressing gradual, mostly benign, AGW. But what happens if the warming is neither gradual nor benign? Various extreme scenarios have been envisaged, from a climate flip (a sudden switch into an ice age resulting from feedback effects following a substantial rise in temperature), to runaway warming (resulting from the release of methane stores beneath frozen peat bogs, the drying and consequent burning of subtropical rainforests, and other factors). How should humanity address such threats?

First, it is worth bearing in mind that climate change is only one of many potential catastrophes awaiting humanity. Others include an asteroid impact and the eruption of a supervolcano (NASA, 2007; Sparks et al., 2005). Such catastrophic events could end all human life. Potentially, all of humanity's available resources could be diverted to attempts to counter these threats. The problem is that in so doing, nothing would be left to address more mundane problems, such as providing clean water, food and shelter.

Taking a less extreme case, some resources could be set aside to address possible catastrophes. Then there would simply be *fewer* resources available to invest in other activities. Clearly, when making decisions about addressing potential future threats, it is necessary to identify such trade-offs and prioritise our actions accordingly.

In the case of potentially catastrophic but highly uncertain climate change (no probability can be assigned because of the chaotic nature of the climate), it seems reasonable to divert a small proportion of investible resources into measures that could reduce the likelihood of such a catastrophe materialising. But how much and into what measures?

Most policy analysts focus primarily on one 'solution': reducing greenhouse gas emissions. But it is not clear that this is the optimal solution. Let us think it through. If rich countries reduce emissions by, say, 5 per cent below 1990 levels – i.e. the Kyoto Protocol commitment but continued indefinitely – this might cost us somewhere between $50 billion and $500 billion a year. Yet, as noted earlier, the impact would be to delay warming by only a few years. Meanwhile, it seems plausible that at some point in the coming century, a dreaded 'tipping point' might still be passed beyond which catastrophe becomes inevitable;

the investment in reducing emissions might delay the onset of the catastrophe by a few years but on its own that would seem to have little real merit. In other words, as the Civil Society Report points out, 'we might end up blowing a trillion dollars and still find ourselves without a planet'.

Meanwhile, if governments took more drastic action to hinder emissions – for example, globally cutting emissions to 20 per cent below 1990 levels by 2020 and keeping them there – the probability of climate catastrophe might be reduced, but only by massively increasingly the likelihood of global economic catastrophe. Indeed, it seems plausible that beyond an economic catastrophe, a global war might result, with those countries seeking to impose carbon constraints fighting with other countries whose populaces refuse to accept such limitations being imposed upon them.

In that light, carbon control per se does not seem like a very smart solution, which is why some analysts have been looking for more acceptable alternatives. Specifically, geoengineering is now being taken seriously as an alternative way of addressing climate catastrophe, should the threat become concrete (Cicerone, 2006; Barrett, 2008). In particular, various relatively low-cost options for either sequestering carbon or reducing incoming solar radiation have been suggested. For example, fertilising the oceans with iron chelate or nitrogen might increase production of plankton, which would absorb carbon dioxide (Markels and Barber, 2001; Boyd, 2004). Meanwhile, firing sulphur into the stratosphere or sending mirrors into space could reduce incoming UV radiation (Crutzen, 2006; NAS, 1991, for mirrors).

These proposals are still speculative and the examples are included here only for illustrative purposes – but they give a sense of what might be possible. Geoengineering technologies are still in their infancy. Much work needs to be done to understand better how they would work and what consequences (both beneficial and adverse) they might have. As to negative impacts, Wigley (2006: 452) points out that the natural experiment represented by the eruption of Mount Pinatubo, which reduced global mean temperatures by around 0.5°C for over a year, did not 'seriously disrupt the climate system', so emitting similar amounts of sulphur artificially should present 'minimal climate risks'. Certainly, geoengineering seems to offer a plausible solution to the possibility of climate catastrophe in a way that attempting to reduce carbon emissions simply does not.

Geoengineering would, however, not be free. Moreover, as with other interventions, it is possible to spend either a great deal or not very much at all. So, how much does it make sense to spend?

Crutzen (2006) cites estimates putting the cost of placing sufficient sulphur into the stratosphere to prevent further warming at between $25 and $50 billion per annum. Others suggest the figure would be closer to $5–$10 billion (Nordhaus, 1994), while one group suggests costs as low as $1 billion (Teller et al., 2003). Even if the cost of preventing catastrophic climate change through geoengineering turns out to be as much as $50 billion/year, that still compares very favourably with many estimates of the cost of the – largely ineffective – Kyoto Protocol.

Note, however, that it is not necessary to begin firing sulphur into the stratosphere just yet, since there is little reason to think that we are close to a tipping point. Also, we may discover that shooting sulphur into the stratosphere is not a very good idea, either because it turns out to have some really bad adverse consequences or because it is more expensive than other options. What does make sense today is to invest in improving our knowledge of the climate system and in developing potential geoengineering systems (Cicerone, 2006). This is similar to the argument for investing in better monitoring of asteroids and in developing technologies that might one day be used to save us from an asteroid impact.

If it is agreed that some investment should be made in geoengineering, both theory and evidence suggest that such development should be carried out by the private sector, regardless of who funds it (we shall come to the funding below). This is simply because private parties would have stronger incentives to identify the most cost-effective schemes than would governments. Consider the analogous case of developing medicines: the private sector has been responsible for developing nearly all the medicines currently in production; by contrast, government investments in the development of medicines have for the most part failed (Morris et al., 2001).

Another important reason for proposing that the development of geoengineering schemes be kept in the private sector – and not directly subsidised – is that by so doing the potential for serious negative consequences is reduced. When government tries to pick winners, it often fails to take into account the negative effects (direct and indirect) of its actions. Perhaps the most spectacular example of this is the diversion – at the behest of the Supreme Soviet – of the rivers running into the Aral Sea. The original reason for the diversion was to irrigate land to grow cotton. This did result in a temporary increase in cotton production, but soon the land became salinified and production stagnated. Meanwhile, the Aral Sea shrank, with much of the delta drying up, devastating local wildlife and fisheries (FAO, 1998).

By contrast, private sector investments tend to be more cautious and carried out with greater concern for the potential negative impacts. This is especially true in countries that have well-functioning systems of private property rights, because property owners engaging in experiments may be held liable for the negative consequences of their actions on other property owners (Morris, 2003).

Why would the private sector make such an investment? For some, it may be an act of pure philanthropy. Bill Gates and Warren Buffett have committed tens of billions of dollars to philanthropic ventures focused on addressing today's most pressing problems. A new generation of entrepreneurs, such as Jeff Skoll (eBay), Larry Page and Sergey Brin (Google), are investing some of their fortunes in projects relating to climate change. Richard Branson (Virgin), too, has set his philanthropic store by climate change. If these philanthropists really believe climate change poses an existential or at least potentially catastrophic threat to humanity, they might do well to ensure that their portfolio of climate change investments includes a geoengineering component.

But it need not be pure philanthropy. Some schemes might become essentially self-financing – even profitable. For example, Michael Markels's proposal to extract carbon dioxide from the atmosphere by fertilising the oceans would potentially increase the amount of fish and other resources (Markels and Barber, 2001). If it were possible to own the rights to the resources thereby produced, some or all of the investment could be recaptured.

Another factor could be the prospect of the issuers of or counterparties to climate-related insurance or bonds utilising geoengineering schemes as a means of mitigating their potential losses. Suppose that a finance company, we'll call it Climate

Speculation Inc. (CSI), has issued a bond that matures on the occurrence of a catastrophic loss associated with AGW. Now, CSI will have an interest in preventing that bond from maturing, so might invest in the development of geoengineering scheme(s). Even if it does not invest in the development of such schemes, it would likely have an interest in using them should the prospect of the catastrophic loss become real – so the mere existence of CSI should incentivise private sector investments in geoengineering.

Another reason investors might invest in the development of geoengineering scheme(s) is the prospect that, at some point in the future, government(s) might purchase their scheme. One way that such a prospect could be made credible would be for government(s) to establish one or more climate catastrophe funds, which, upon a specified set of criteria linked to approaching climate catastrophe (e.g. Lenton et al., 2008), would be used to purchase proven geoengineering projects that could avert the catastrophe(s).

To the extent that the threat of catastrophe is a result of human emissions of various greenhouse gases, the ethically desirable solution might arguably be for the individuals and businesses emitting such gases to pay in proportion to their emissions.[2] In practice, this may be difficult to achieve, since it would entail monitoring the emissions of over six billion people, including all their agricultural and industrial activities.

---

2   If we were to look at this from the perspective of standard welfare economics, we could also add that in the face of uncertainty over future benefits and in the context of a relatively steep short-run marginal social cost curve, there is a prima facie case for charging for, rather than imposing a cap on, emissions.

A proposal

There is now a pressing demand in rich countries to 'do something' about climate change. Moreover, the policy idea that is most widely discussed is the imposition of caps on emissions of greenhouse gases. This is worrying because there is a potential for very substantial harm to be done through the imposition of such caps, while the likelihood of equivalent or greater benefit is small. We have already seen enormous damage as a result of the attempt to implement the Kyoto Protocol, which sought to impose a very modest cap on industrial-country emissions. A tighter cap could be catastrophic, especially given the likely knock-on effects of trade sanctions and industry-specific initiatives that seem inevitable once the horse trading begins in legislatures.

So, here is a proposal. Burning carbon-based fuels and making cement currently account for the majority of the approximately eight gigatons of carbon dioxide emissions humans emit into the atmosphere (Marland et al., 2007). If a tax of $1 were applied to each ton of emissions that would raise approximately US$8 billion per year.[3] If only emissions in wealthy countries were taxed, the

---

3   Environmental economists argue that the tax should be levied at a rate equal to the marginal social cost of carbon at the point where the marginal cost equals the marginal benefit. In practice, uncertainties over both costs and benefits make precise calculation of this figure impossible. Nevertheless, economists have attempted to provide estimates. Tol (2005) analysed many of these estimates and found that the mean was $16/tC, the median was $7/tC and the mode was $2/tC. When he recalculated the estimates for different discount rates and various probabilistic models (to account for different ways of analysing the potential for catastrophe), he found a 'certainty equivalent' price of $25/tC (assuming a pure rate of time preference of 3 per cent) (Tol, 2007). Tol's estimates assume, however, that the only way to reduce the likelihood of catastrophic warming is to reduce carbon concentrations. If geoengineering is included as an option, we could instead take the cost of implementing geoengineering as the backstop price.

amount raised would be around US$5 billion per year.[4] If some part of such taxes were hypothecated to climate catastrophe funds, it could be argued that they were in fact a form of insurance.[5] In addition, the tax itself will raise the price of carbon-based fuels and thereby incentivise the development of lower-carbon fuels and other carbon-reducing technologies.

Ross McKitrick (2008) makes a convincing case that the rate of any carbon tax should vary in proportion to the putative harm. Specifically, he suggests a tax that would vary according to changes in temperature in the tropical troposphere, a part of the atmosphere that is thought to be particularly susceptible to AGW. In order to reduce the variability of tax rates, Dr McKitrick suggests taking a three-year moving average of those temperatures. In addition to raising revenue and promoting lower-carbon technologies, such a tax would encourage private sector investment in climate forecasting, since companies would want to know how high the tax is likely to be in the future, so they can calculate how much to invest in new technologies, energy efficiency improvements, and so on.

A 'T3 tax', as suggested by McKitrick, set initially at $1 per ton of carbon dioxide and applied at a national level in wealthy

---

4   It was pointed out by an anonymous referee that the introduction of a carbon tax in wealthy countries would result in a shift in production of energy-intensive goods to poorer countries. This is no doubt true at the margin. If the carbon tax rate is kept low, however, the proportion of businesses that relocate purely on the basis of the tax is likely to be small.

5   A question inevitably arises as to what should happen to the funds if no climate catastrophe arises within a reasonable time frame (e.g. twenty years) and it becomes clear that none is likely ever to occur. In that case, the funds could be diverted – for example, to paying off government debt. This is a good enough reason in itself to keep such funds under the direct control of national governments and not entrust them to some unaccountable intergovernmental bureaucracy.

countries, would be an ideal way to raise funds to support a combination of enhanced monitoring and modelling of the climate and investments in geoengineering. The tax could be varied so that if the warming in the tropical troposphere indicated that temperatures were approaching a tipping point, the rate would increase – thereby providing more money for the catastrophe funds. It also seems likely that if temperatures really did rise dramatically, poorer countries might also introduce their own carbon taxes and catastrophe funds, thereby reducing the likelihood that industries would be substantially diverted in order to avoid paying the carbon tax. Of course, if the temperature at the tropical troposphere fell, then the tax rate would fall.

Conclusions

I have argued that the relationship between human emissions of greenhouse gases (GHGs) and global warming remains uncertain. Plausibly, increased emissions of GHGs during the 21st century will lead to mild warming – of perhaps 1–3° Celsius. To the extent that this warming occurs gradually, the best strategy is likely to be adaptation. The appropriate policy response under such circumstances is to reduce barriers to adaptation, such as regulatory restrictions and taxes that inhibit the free flow of information and thereby prevent entrepreneurs from identifying and seeking to fill market niches.

There remains a possibility, however, that more catastrophic warming might occur. Given the difficulty and cost of attempting to reduce emissions on a global scale, one strategy to address this remote catastrophic risk is to invest in geoengineering. Such investments would ideally come from the private sector, motivated either by philanthropy or the potential for profit – or some combination of the two.

To the extent that there is a role for government to 'insure' against catastrophe, it is proposed that some individual national governments might introduce small taxes on carbon-based energies. Such taxes might be linked to the temperature at the tropical troposphere, or some other (set of) leading indicators of potential catastrophe. If the leading indicators show strongly that a catastrophe is imminent, the funds thereby obtained could then be used to pay for geoengineering. Such taxes would also provide modest incentives to develop and use lower-carbon energy technologies. As noted, the geoengineering solutions discussed in this chapter are not intended to be specific recommendations to be adopted if a tipping point is reached: rather, they are indications of the sort of solutions that might be possible. Indeed, if history is a guide, it is likely that in the future new, as yet unknown, technologies will offer superior, less costly ways of addressing whatever problems materialise. So, while vigilance is essential and research into potential solutions desirable, the primary response should remain 'wait and see'. Note also that this policy proposal is not intended to be somehow 'optimal'. Given the institutional constraints on implementing any proposal for addressing such a complex issue, it would be folly indeed to pretend otherwise. Instead, the proposal is put forward as one that is both politically feasible and economically viable.

References

Arbogast, K. B., M. J. Kallan and D. R. Durbin (2005),
    'Effectiveness of high back and backless belt-positioning

booster seats in side impact crashes', *Annual Proceedings of the Association of Advancement of Automotive Medicine*, 49: 201–13.

Attaran, A., D. R. Roberts, C. F. Curtis and W. L. Kilama (2000), 'Balancing risks on the backs of the poor', *Nature Medicine*, 6: 729–31.

Barrett, S. (2008), 'The incredible economics of geoengineering', *Environment and Resource Economics*, 39: 45–54.

Boyd, P. (2004), 'Ironing out algal issues in the Southern Ocean', *Science*, 304(5669): 396–7.

Cicerone, R. J. (2006), 'Geoengineering: encouraging research and overseeing implementation', *Climate Change*, 77: 221–6.

Crutzen, P. (2006), 'Albedo enhancement by stratospheric sulfur injections: a contribution to resolve a policy dilemma?', *Climatic Change*, 77(3/4): 211–20.

Durbin, D. R., M. R. Elliott and F. K. Winston (2003), 'Belt-positioning booster seats and reduction in risk of injury among children in vehicle crashes', *Journal of the American Medical Association*, 289(21): 2835–40.

Dye, C. and P. Reiter (2000), 'Climate change and malaria: temperatures without fevers', *Science*, 289(5485): 1697–8.

Emanuel, K. (2005a), 'Increasing destructiveness of tropical cyclones over the past 30 years', *Nature*, 436: 686–88.

Emanuel, K. (2005b), 'Emanuel replies', *Nature*, 438: E13.

Epstein, P. R. (1998), 'Global warming and vector-borne disease', *The Lancet*, 351(9117): 1737.

FAO (1998), 'Time to save the Aral Sea?', *Spotlight*, Rome: UN Food and Agricultural Organization, available at: www.fao.org/Ag/Magazine/9809/spot2.htm.

Goklany, I. (2007), *Climate Change and Extreme Weather Events*, Civil Society Coalition on Climate Change Working Paper.

Goldenberg et al. (2001), 'The recent increase in Atlantic hurricane activity: causes and implications', *Science*, 293(5529): 474–9.

Green, K. C. and J. S. Armstrong (forthcoming), 'Global warming: forecasts by scientists versus scientific forecasts', *Energy and Environment.*

Haines, A. and J. A. Patz (2004), 'Health effects of climate change', *Journal of the American Medical Association*, 291: 99–103.

Houghton, J. (2005), *Global Warming: The Complete Briefing*, Cambridge: Cambridge University Press.

Keatinge, W. (2004), 'Illness and mortality from heat and cold: will global warming matter?', in Okonski and Morris (eds), *Environment and Health – Myths and Realities*, London: International Policy Press.

Landsea, C. (2005), 'Hurricanes and global warming', *Nature*, 438: E11–13.

Lenton, T. M., H. Held, E. Kriegler, J. W. Hall, W. Lucht, S. Rahmstorf and H. J. Schellnhuber (2008), 'Tipping elements in the Earth's climate system', *Proceedings of the National Academy of Sciences*, 105(6): 1786–93.

Lindzen, R. (2005), 'The economics of climate change', Memorandum by Professor Richard S. Lindzen, Massachusetts Institute of Technology, House of Lords Select Committee on Economic Affairs, 2nd Report of Session 2005–2006, vol. II, pp. 44–55.

Lomborg, B. (2001), *The Sceptical Environmentalist: Measuring the Real State of the World*, Cambridge: Cambridge University Press.

Mann, M. E., R. S. Bradley and M. K. Hughes (1998), 'Global-scale temperature patterns and climate forcing over the past six centuries', *Nature*, 392: 779–87.

Mann, M. E., R. S. Bradley and M. K. Hughes (1999), 'Northern hemisphere temperatures during the past millennium: inferences, uncertainties, and limitations', *Geophysical Research Letters*, 26(6): 759–62.

Markels, M. and R. T. Barber (2001), 'Sequestration of CO_2 by ocean fertilization', Poster presentation for NETL Conference on Carbon Sequestration, 14–17 May.

Marland, G., T. A. Boden and R. J. Andres (2007), *Global, Regional, and National CO_2 Emissions*. In *Trends: A Compendium of Data on Global Change*, Carbon Dioxide Information Analysis Center, Oak Ridge National Laboratory, US Department of Energy, Oak Ridge, TN.

McIntyre, S. and R. McKitrick (2003), 'Corrections to the Mann et al. (1998) proxy data base and northern hemisphere average temperature series', *Energy and Environment*, 14(6): 751–72.

McKitrick, R. (2008), 'The T3 tax as a policy strategy for global warming', in A. Nakamura (ed.), *The Vancouver Volumes*, Vancouver, BC: Trafford Press.

Moore, V. M., J. Dolinnis and A. J. Woodward (1995), 'Vehicle speed and risk of a severe crash', *Epidemiology*, 6(3): 258–62.

Morris, J. (2003), 'Climbing out of the hole: sunsets, subjective value, the environment and English common law', *Fordham Environmental Law Journal*, XIV(2).

Morris, J., R. Mowett, W. D. Reekie and R. Tren (2001), *Ideal Matter: Globalisation and the Intellectual Property Debate*, Brussels: Centre for the New Europe.

Morrison, D. S. (2001), 'Reducing speed limit to 20 mph in urban areas: evidence based principles should be applied to non-health sector interventions', *British Medical Journal*, 322(7277): 50.

NAS (National Academy of Sciences) (1991), *Policy Implications of Greenhouse Warming – Synthesis Panel Report*, Washington, DC: National Academy Press.

NASA (National Aeronautics and Space Administration) (2007), *List of Potentially Hazardous Asteroids (PHAs)*, NASA Near Earth Object Program.

Nordhaus, W. D. (1994), *Managing the Global Commons: The Economics of Climate Change*, Cambridge, MA: MIT Press.

Patz, J. A., M. Hulme, C. Rosenzweig, T. D. Mitchell, R. A. Goldberg, A. K. Githeko, S. Lele, A. J. McMichael and D. Le Sueur (2002), 'Climate change (communication arising): regional warming and malaria resurgence', *Nature*, 420: 627.

Pielke, R., Jr (2005), 'Are there trends in hurricane destruction?', *Nature*, 438: E11.

Rayner, S. and E. S. Malone (eds) (1998), *Human Choice and Climate Change*, vol. 3: *The Tools for Policy Analysis*, Columbus, OH: Batelle Press.

Reiter, P. (2001), 'Climate change and mosquito borne disease', *Environmental Health Perspectives Supplements*, 109(S1), March.

Reiter, P. (2005), 'Climate change and Highland malaria in the tropics', Poster presented at DEFRA Conference on Avoiding Dangerous Climate Change.

Reiter, P. (2007), *Human Ecology and Human Behavior: Climate change and health in perspective*, Civil Society Coalition on Climate Change Working Paper.

Roberts, D. R., S. Manguin and J. Mouchet (2000), 'DDT house spraying and re-emerging malaria', *The Lancet*, 356: 330–32.

Southgate, D. and B. Songhen (2007), *Weathering Global Warming in Agriculture and Forestry: It Can be Done with Free Markets*, Civil Society Coalition on Climate Change Working Paper.

Sparks, S., S. Self, J. Grattan, C. Oppenheimer, D. Pyle and H. Rymer (2005), *Super-eruptions: Global effects and future threats*, Report of a Geological Society of London Working Group, 2nd print edn.

Stern, N. et al. (2006), *Stern Review: The Economics of Climate Change*, London: HM Treasury.

Teller, E., R. Hyde, M. Ishikawa, J. Nuckolls and L. Wood (2003), 'Active stabilization of climate: inexpensive, low risk, near-term options for preventing global warming and ice ages via technologically varied solar radiative forcing,' Lawrence Livermore National Library, 30 November.

Tol, R. S. J. (2005), 'The marginal damage costs of carbon dioxide emissions: an assessment of the uncertainties', *Energy Policy*, 33: 2064–74.

Tol, R. S. J. (2007), 'The social cost of carbon: trends, outliers and catastrophes', *Economics E-Journal* Discussion Paper 2007–44, available at: www.economics-ejournal.org/economics/discussionpapers.

Vecchi, G. A. and B. J. Soden (2007), 'Increased tropical Atlantic wind shear in model projections of global warming', *Geophys. Res. Lett.*, 34, L08702.

Watson, R. et al. (2001), *Climate Change 2001: Synthesis Report*, Cambridge: Cambridge University Press.

Wegman, E., D. W. Scott and Y. H. Said (2006), *National Ad Hoc Committee Report on the 'Hockey Stick' Global Climate*

Reconstruction ('The Wegman Report'), Washington, DC: US House Committee on Energy and Commerce.

WHO (World Health Organisation) (2005), 'Climate and health fact sheet', July.

WHO (2006), 'WHO gives indoor use of DDT a clean bill of health for controlling malaria', WHO News Release, 15 September.

Wigley, T. M. L. (2006), 'A combined mitigation/geoengineering approach to climate stabilization', *Science*, 314: 452–4.

ABOUT THE IEA

The Institute is a research and educational charity (No. CC 235 351), limited by guarantee. Its mission is to improve understanding of the fundamental institutions of a free society by analysing and expounding the role of markets in solving economic and social problems.

The IEA achieves its mission by:

- a high-quality publishing programme
- conferences, seminars, lectures and other events
- outreach to school and college students
- brokering media introductions and appearances

The IEA, which was established in 1955 by the late Sir Antony Fisher, is an educational charity, not a political organisation. It is independent of any political party or group and does not carry on activities intended to affect support for any political party or candidate in any election or referendum, or at any other time. It is financed by sales of publications, conference fees and voluntary donations.

In addition to its main series of publications the IEA also publishes a quarterly journal, *Economic Affairs*.

The IEA is aided in its work by a distinguished international Academic Advisory Council and an eminent panel of Honorary Fellows. Together with other academics, they review prospective IEA publications, their comments being passed on anonymously to authors. All IEA papers are therefore subject to the same rigorous independent refereeing process as used by leading academic journals.

IEA publications enjoy widespread classroom use and course adoptions in schools and universities. They are also sold throughout the world and often translated/reprinted.

Since 1974 the IEA has helped to create a worldwide network of 100 similar institutions in over 70 countries. They are all independent but share the IEA's mission.

Views expressed in the IEA's publications are those of the authors, not those of the Institute (which has no corporate view), its Managing Trustees, Academic Advisory Council members or senior staff.

Members of the Institute's Academic Advisory Council, Honorary Fellows, Trustees and Staff are listed on the following page.

The Institute gratefully acknowledges financial support for its publications programme and other work from a generous benefaction by the late Alec and Beryl Warren.

161

Other papers recently published by the IEA include:

WHO, What and Why?
Transnational Government, Legitimacy and the World Health Organization
Roger Scruton
Occasional Paper 113; ISBN 0 255 36487 3; £8.00

The World Turned Rightside Up
A New Trading Agenda for the Age of Globalisation
John C. Hulsman
Occasional Paper 114; ISBN 0 255 36495 4; £8.00

The Representation of Business in English Literature
Introduced and edited by Arthur Pollard
Readings 53; ISBN 0 255 36491 1; £12.00

Anti-Liberalism 2000
The Rise of New Millennium Collectivism
David Henderson
Occasional Paper 115; ISBN 0 255 36497 0; £7.50

Capitalism, Morality and Markets
Brian Griffiths, Robert A. Sirico, Norman Barry & Frank Field
Readings 54; ISBN 0 255 36496 2; £7.50

A Conversation with Harris and Seldon
Ralph Harris & Arthur Seldon
Occasional Paper 116; ISBN 0 255 36498 9; £7.50

Malaria and the DDT Story
Richard Tren & Roger Bate
Occasional Paper 117; ISBN 0 255 36499 7; £10.00

A Plea to Economists Who Favour Liberty: Assist the Everyman
Daniel B. Klein
Occasional Paper 118; ISBN 0 255 36501 2; £10.00

HIV and Aids in Schools
The Political Economy of Pressure Groups and Miseducation
Barrie Craven, Pauline Dixon, Gordon Stewart & James Tooley
Occasional Paper 121; ISBN 0 255 36522 5; £10.00

The Road to Serfdom
The Reader's Digest *condensed version*
Friedrich A. Hayek
Occasional Paper 122; ISBN 0 255 36530 6; £7.50

Bastiat's *The Law*
Introduction by Norman Barry
Occasional Paper 123; ISBN 0 255 36509 8; £7.50

A Globalist Manifesto for Public Policy
Charles Calomiris
Occasional Paper 124; ISBN 0 255 36525 X; £7.50

Euthanasia for Death Duties
Putting Inheritance Tax Out of Its Misery
Barry Bracewell-Milnes
Research Monograph 54; ISBN 0 255 36513 6; £10.00

Liberating the Land
The Case for Private Land-use Planning
Mark Pennington
Hobart Paper 143; ISBN 0 255 36508 X; £10.00

IEA Yearbook of Government Performance 2002/2003
Edited by Peter Warburton
Yearbook 1; ISBN 0 255 36532 2; £15.00

Britain's Relative Economic Performance, 1870–1999
Nicholas Crafts
Research Monograph 55; ISBN 0 255 36524 1; £10.00

Should We Have Faith in Central Banks?
Otmar Issing
Occasional Paper 125; ISBN 0 255 36528 4; £7.50

The Dilemma of Democracy
Arthur Seldon
Hobart Paper 136 (reissue); ISBN 0 255 36536 5; £10.00

Capital Controls: a 'Cure' Worse Than the Problem?
Forrest Capie
Research Monograph 56; ISBN 0 255 36506 3; £10.00

The Poverty of 'Development Economics'
Deepak Lal
Hobart Paper 144 (reissue); ISBN 0 255 36519 5; £15.00

Should Britain Join the Euro?
The Chancellor's Five Tests Examined
Patrick Minford
Occasional Paper 126; ISBN 0 255 36527 6; £7.50

Post-Communist Transition: Some Lessons
Leszek Balcerowicz
Occasional Paper 127; ISBN 0 255 36533 0; £7.50

A Tribute to Peter Bauer
John Blundell et al.
Occasional Paper 128; ISBN 0 255 36531 4; £10.00

Employment Tribunals
Their Growth and the Case for Radical Reform
J. R. Shackleton
Hobart Paper 145; ISBN 0 255 36515 2; £10.00

Fifty Economic Fallacies Exposed
Geoffrey E. Wood
Occasional Paper 129; ISBN 0 255 36518 7; £12.50

A Market in Airport Slots
Keith Boyfield (editor), David Starkie, Tom Bass & Barry Humphreys
Readings 56; ISBN 0 255 36505 5; £10.00

Money, Inflation and the Constitutional Position of the Central Bank
Milton Friedman & Charles A. E. Goodhart
Readings 57; ISBN 0 255 36538 1; £10.00

railway.com
Parallels between the Early British Railways and the ICT Revolution
Robert C. B. Miller
Research Monograph 57; ISBN 0 255 36534 9; £12.50

The Regulation of Financial Markets
Edited by Philip Booth & David Currie
Readings 58; ISBN 0 255 36551 9; £12.50

Climate Alarmism Reconsidered
Robert L. Bradley Jr
Hobart Paper 146; ISBN 0 255 36541 1; £12.50

Government Failure: E. G. West on Education
Edited by James Tooley & James Stanfield
Occasional Paper 130; ISBN 0 255 36552 7; £12.50

Corporate Governance: Accountability in the Marketplace
Elaine Sternberg
Second edition
Hobart Paper 147; ISBN 0 255 36542 X; £12.50

The Land Use Planning System
Evaluating Options for Reform
John Corkindale
Hobart Paper 148; ISBN 0 255 36550 0; £10.00

Economy and Virtue
Essays on the Theme of Markets and Morality
Edited by Dennis O'Keeffe
Readings 59; ISBN 0 255 36504 7; £12.50

Free Markets Under Siege
Cartels, Politics and Social Welfare
Richard A. Epstein
Occasional Paper 132; ISBN 0 255 36553 5; £10.00

Unshackling Accountants
D. R. Myddelton
Hobart Paper 149; ISBN 0 255 36559 4; £12.50

The Euro as Politics
Pedro Schwartz
Research Monograph 58; ISBN 0 255 36535 7; £12.50

Pricing Our Roads
Vision and Reality
Stephen Glaister & Daniel J. Graham
Research Monograph 59; ISBN 0 255 36562 4; £10.00

The Role of Business in the Modern World
Progress, Pressures, and Prospects for the Market Economy
David Henderson
Hobart Paper 150; ISBN 0 255 36548 9; £12.50

Public Service Broadcasting Without the BBC?
Alan Peacock
Occasional Paper 133; ISBN 0 255 36565 9; £10.00

The ECB and the Euro: the First Five Years
Otmar Issing
Occasional Paper 134; ISBN 0 255 36555 1; £10.00

Towards a Liberal Utopia?
Edited by Philip Booth
Hobart Paperback 32; ISBN 0 255 36563 2; £15.00

The Way Out of the Pensions Quagmire
Philip Booth & Deborah Cooper
Research Monograph 60; ISBN 0 255 36517 9; £12.50

Black Wednesday
A Re-examination of Britain's Experience in the Exchange Rate Mechanism
Alan Budd
Occasional Paper 135; ISBN 0 255 36566 7; £7.50

Crime: Economic Incentives and Social Networks
Paul Ormerod
Hobart Paper 151; ISBN 0 255 36554 3; £10.00

The Road to Serfdom *with* **The Intellectuals and Socialism**
Friedrich A. Hayek
Occasional Paper 136; ISBN 0 255 36576 4; £10.00

Money and Asset Prices in Boom and Bust
Tim Congdon
Hobart Paper 152; ISBN 0 255 36570 5; £10.00

The Dangers of Bus Re-regulation
and Other Perspectives on Markets in Transport
John Hibbs et al.
Occasional Paper 137; ISBN 0 255 36572 1; £10.00

The New Rural Economy
Change, Dynamism and Government Policy
Berkeley Hill et al.
Occasional Paper 138; ISBN 0 255 36546 2; £15.00

The Benefits of Tax Competition
Richard Teather
Hobart Paper 153; ISBN 0 255 36569 1; £12.50

Wheels of Fortune
Self-funding Infrastructure and the Free Market Case for a Land Tax
Fred Harrison
Hobart Paper 154; ISBN 0 255 36589 6; £12.50

Were 364 Economists All Wrong?
Edited by Philip Booth
Readings 60; ISBN 978 0 255 36588 8; £10.00

Europe After the 'No' Votes
Mapping a New Economic Path
Patrick A. Messerlin
Occasional Paper 139; ISBN 978 0 255 36580 2; £10.00

The Railways, the Market and the Government
John Hibbs et al.
Readings 61; ISBN 978 0 255 36567 3; £12.50

Corruption: The World's Big C
Cases, Causes, Consequences, Cures
Ian Senior
Research Monograph 61; ISBN 978 0 255 36571 0; £12.50

Choice and the End of Social Housing
Peter King
Hobart Paper 155; ISBN 978 0 255 36568 0; £10.00

Sir Humphrey's Legacy
Facing Up to the Cost of Public Sector Pensions
Neil Record
Hobart Paper 156; ISBN 978 0 255 36578 9; £10.00

The Economics of Law
Cento Veljanovski
Second edition
Hobart Paper 157; ISBN 978 0 255 36561 1; £12.50

Living with Leviathan
Public Spending, Taxes and Economic Performance
David B. Smith
Hobart Paper 158; ISBN 978 0 255 36579 6; £12.50

The Vote Motive
Gordon Tullock
New edition
Hobart Paperback 33; ISBN 978 0 255 36577 2; £10.00

Waging the War of Ideas
John Blundell
Third edition
Occasional Paper 131; ISBN 978 0 255 36606 9; £12.50

The War Between the State and the Family
How Government Divides and Impoverishes
Patricia Morgan
Hobart Paper 159; ISBN 978 0 255 36596 3; £10.00

Capitalism – A Condensed Version
Arthur Seldon
Occasional Paper 140; ISBN 978 0 255 36598 7; £7.50

Catholic Social Teaching and the Market Economy
Edited by Philip Booth
Hobart Paperback 34; ISBN 978 0 255 36581 9; £15.00

Adam Smith – A Primer
Eamonn Butler
Occasional Paper 141; ISBN 978 0 255 36608 3; £7.50

Happiness, Economics and Public Policy
Helen Johns & Paul Ormerod
Research Monograph 62; ISBN 978 0 255 36600 7; £10.00

They Meant Well
Government Project Disasters
D. R. Myddelton
Hobart Paper 160; ISBN 978 0 255 36601 4; £12.50

Rescuing Social Capital from Social Democracy
John Meadowcroft & Mark Pennington
Hobart Paper 161; ISBN 978 0 255 36592 5; £10.00

Paths to Property
Approaches to Institutional Change in International Development
Karol Boudreaux & Paul Dragos Aligica
Hobart Paper 162; ISBN 978 0 255 36582 6; £10.00

Prohibitions
Edited by John Meadowcroft
Hobart Paperback 35; ISBN 978 0 255 36585 7; £15.00

Trade Policy, New Century
The WTO, FTAs and Asia Rising
Razeen Sally
Hobart Paper 163; ISBN 978 0 255 36544 4; £12.50

Sixty Years On – Who Cares for the NHS?
Helen Evans
Research Monograph 63; ISBN 978 0 255 36611 3; £10.00

Taming Leviathan
Waging the War of Ideas Around the World
Edited by Colleen Dyble
Occasional Paper 142; ISBN 978 0 255 36607 6; £12.50

The Legal Foundations of Free Markets
Edited by Stephen F. Copp
Hobart Paperback 36; ISBN 978 0 255 36591 8; £15.00

Other IEA publications

Comprehensive information on other publications and the wider work of the IEA can be found at www.iea.org.uk. To order any publication please see below.

Personal customers

Orders from personal customers should be directed to the IEA:
Bob Layson
IEA
2 Lord North Street
FREEPOST LON10168
London SW1P 3YZ
Tel: 020 7799 8909. Fax: 020 7799 2137
Email: blayson@iea.org.uk

Trade customers

All orders from the book trade should be directed to the IEA's distributor:
Gazelle Book Services Ltd (IEA Orders)
FREEPOST RLYS-EAHU-YSCZ
White Cross Mills
Hightown
Lancaster LA1 4XS
Tel: 01524 68765, Fax: 01524 53232
Email: sales@gazellebooks.co.uk

IEA subscriptions

The IEA also offers a subscription service to its publications. For a single annual payment (currently £42.00 in the UK), subscribers receive every monograph the IEA publishes. For more information please contact:
Adam Myers
Subscriptions
IEA
2 Lord North Street
FREEPOST LON10168
London SW1P 3YZ
Tel: 020 7799 8920, Fax: 020 7799 2137
Email: amyers@iea.org.uk